101 ADVENTURES IN SAUDI ARABIA

AND

PASSAGE TO JERUSALEM

5-18-08
Claire W. Schumacher

by

CLAIRE W. SCHUMACHER

Zenith publications
#28 Holly Lane,
Duluth Minnesota 55810

Printed in the United States of America

LIBRARY OF CONGRESS CATALOGUE NUMBER
94-090015

ISBN   0-917378-08-3

Photographs by Claire W. Schumacher

Dedicated to Karl and
Margaret who made this
incredible journey possible.

Karl was deceased on
December 18, 1985, in
Jiddah, Saudi Arabia,
age 50 years.
His remains were buried
in the Red Sea on July 4, 1986.
He is much missed by all of
his family and many friends.
His life was a true adventure
in living life to its fullest
and with his values intact.
In loving memory from
sister Claire.

BOOK I

101 ADVENTURES

IN

SAUDI ARABIA

CONTENTS

CONTINUED...........

CHAPTER I

SAUDI ARABIA--BEFORE THE GULF WAR

Near midnight, the giant Air France 747 jet soared over the Red Sea, having passed over the pyramids of Egypt earlier in the evening and safely crossed thousands of sand-filled miles over the unconquerable Sahara. Jiddah or Jeddah (we will use Jiddah), Saudi Arabia, "the Bride of the Red Sea," bedecked in her crown of jewels, loomed out of that terrible blackness that engulfs the Mideast. I peered out of the small window, shivering in fear and anticipation, realizing this ancient City is purportedly the burial place of man's common ancestor, Eve. Yes, the "Eve" of "Adam and--" I had gained nine hours of time. Midnight here when I would land was mid-afternoon back home in Proctor, Minnesota, in the heartland of America.

As we descended, the pilot announced we couldn't bring any newspapers or magazines into the City and cameras must be put away in our suitcases. I looked around at the other passengers with curiosity. I had found only one who spoke English on this plane and he was from England. I shook my head in amazement as I realized that Aladdin's lamp of long ago really had nothing on our jet age of today.

Only this morning I had boarded the airplane in Paris. All through the sunny day we had flown south over Europe, where, even in early February, the land was free of snow, except over the Alps. I had seen the snow-covered tops of the awesome, legendary mountains that were so far below that they looked minute and it was difficult to realize that these were the mighty Alps that defied man's ascent to their summit. I had turned around in my seat to see if there was anyone to share the sight of the quaint little villages nestled in the wrinkles of Old Man Mountain.

At this time there were still some English-speaking passengers, but they were not alone, as I was, and seemed wrapped up in conversation with their companions. More alone than ever, without anyone to converse with, I strained to peer below, marveling at the long stringlike roads engraved across the enormous expanse of the rocky mountain chain. The winding road led to distant villages in other hidden crevices that made me wonder if anyone ever escaped from there.

I had guessed we were over Italy, but I couldn't see the Vatican, nor even Rome. Then we were out over the sea. After a period of time I saw the first sprinkling of islands and wondered if these spatters of land in the waters were part of ancient Greece. Sometime later, as night had almost closed in on Athens, we landed on that famous island. Fog and twilight hung over it, and I searched in vain for a sight of the ancient ruins that I had heard of all my life. Little did I know that in a few years my mother would die from a heart attack on this very island.

We stopped only long enough to discharge passengers. All of the English speaking people deplaned now. We took on some Greek airline hostesses with dark eyes and hair and an English accent hard to understand when they spoke over the intercom.

Off again. In just minutes we had left Athens where we could see car lights on the outer edges of the island, perhaps going home from work. Now over the Aegean Sea, night settled in and there was nothing to see except extreme blackness out the window.

As we winged our way in the giant plane toward Egypt, I wondered how this could actually be me, an American housewife of little means, who, until a few months ago had never dreamed in her wildest fancies that she would ever visit this ancient land of Biblical lore.

My brother, Karl Wombacher, had written me a letter, which, when I read it almost caused me to faint right out of my kitchen chair in small town Proctor, Minnesota. After the first few paragraphs, I came to this statement, "Margaret and I would like you to come visit us. Would this be possible if we sent you a ticket to fly here?" Go to Jiddah, Saudi Arabia? I laughed at first when I read it even while shivers played havoc on my arm and spine. The laughter turned into a bemused question and the answer eventually landed me in this airplane.

It hadn't been easy. My husband and two children didn't really sanction the idea. It was difficult to get away from work at the University for a month and, financially, it was next to impossible to raise the money for the trip, even though the ticket was free. But I knew I couldn't pass up this once-in-a-lifetime venture. No one else knew what I had to do in my lifetime--only I could decide that, I thought.

Suddenly dim lights loomed out of the night. The pilot announced in a deeply French accent that we were about to land in Cairo. Imagine! I strained my eyes hoping somehow to see more of this legendary city of the Pharaohs, Cleopatra and the pyramids. The lights were dim and mysterious. I shivered, feeling alone and frightened. Never having flown before, I had been very scared at the prospect of this trip. I even made out a will, half anticipating that I'd never return home again. Arabia just seemed too far away to deal with in my mind. In spite of my fear, I still had to go because that's my nature--not to let opportunity escape.

While on my way to the washroom I almost collided with a portly middle-aged man. I wanted to hug him when he apologized in English--the King's English. By this time I was so grateful to find another human being who spoke my language. I had experienced the agony of not speaking the same language when I wandered around Paris for three days, awaiting my flight to Jiddah. I realized then how primary language was in finding my way around this planet, that it is the thing that elevates us above the animals--we could communicate ideas. And when I couldn't speak to any of the Frenchmen, I was deprived of my greatest traveling asset.

"You speak English!" I exclaimed in relief.

"So do you," the man laughed, implying he understood my meaning. We talked for a minute and later, on the plane he came and sat beside me, which seemed perfectly normal, like a gathering of hometown people when no one else could speak with me.

"I'm Charley Musker," he said. He explained his dark graying hair and dark eyes by saying he was half Greek and half English, having been born in Athens, but educated in England. He now lived mainly in Cambridge, England, where he had a wife and grown son. However, his employment took him to Arabia occasionally and he worked there for months at a time. "I'm a buyer for an architectural firm," he explained in his dignified English accent. We talked on and on until suddenly, as I glanced out the window, I could see pinpoints of light in the distance of the terrible blackness outside, not realizing until later when I was leaving Arabia that we had been flying over the vast Sahara for many hours and then across the Red Sea. Jiddah was in sight! My heart almost stood still with fear which only the prospect of the yawning gulf of the unknown future engenders. I hardly heard Charlie Musker as he said, "I'll be staying on the English compound. If after a few days, you'd have your brother look me up, (I obviously didn't know where Karl lived), perhaps we could do some sightseeing together.

I said I'd certainly keep it in mind--the pilot was announcing our approaching landing. Exactly midnight was the time as I gathered my things together and prepared to disembark in Saudi Arabia, well into the advent of my great adventure.

"Leave all magazines and newspapers on the plane," our pilot announced. "All cameras must be locked in your suitcase." I pulled out my small camera and snapped a forbidden picture as we approached the airport. Even then I thought of a name for that picture if it turned out--"Land in the Shadow"--

Waiting in line with foreigners of many nationalities in their native garb, I wondered if Karl had received my letter telling him when I would arrive. What if he wasn't there to meet me? My heart skipped a beat. Letter delivery was uncertain, at best, and I had addressed mine only to a P.O. box. I knew they had no telephone, so I would really be lost if he wasn't in the terminal. I immersed myself in the deplaning crowd and walked into the airport. I frantically searched the small crowd in vain for the face of Karl with his brown hair, freckled face and glasses, standing 6'3", all of which labeled him the intellectual English teacher that he was. I had lost track of my only English contact by this time. Dark, hostile eyes looked at me almost accusingly as the Arabian men watched us get off the plane. I felt like I was the only blue-eyed red-head in the world. Later, I realized that Moslem/Arabian women are not allowed out on the street alone, much less at midnight in the airport. When they do go out they must be veiled from head to toe.

With trepidation, I watched the long robed immigration authorities search my handbag. My suitcase had already been "lost" between Duluth, Minnesota and Chicago, Illinois and I was afraid it would never arrive--a whole month without my clothes was a real and frightening possibility. Just then I looked toward the door and saw my wonderful younger brother grinning from ear to ear at me.

He was talking to the young immigration men, whom I later found had been two of his students. He was their English teacher, having been hired by TWA to teach English to the Arabian Airline employees. Their demeanor was much friendlier when they gave back my things after Karl told them I was his sister.

I hugged him, happy for more than one reason to see my brother. I was puzzled that he was surprised to see me. I asked him if he had gotten my letter. He hadn't.

"But, he explained, I've been checking the midnight flights this week. There are only two a week from Paris. "I hadn't gone to bed yet and I thought I'd run over to the airport in case you would happen to be on this plane."

"Thank God, you did," I gulped, not knowing what would have happened to me otherwise.

"We weren't even sure you were coming," he explained. This statement was later to make more sense to me as I was quickly indoctrinated into the isolationism of the Americans here in Jeddah. They almost forget there is an outside world, they are so insulated.

We got out of the airport fast. It was later to be modernized, but at that time it was small and easy to get out of. We climbed into Karl's compact car. It was a short ride to the "American compound" (there were five scattered all over the huge sprawling City of Jiddah).This one was commonly known as the "old TWA compound". During this ride after midnight, I hadn't yet gotten the full impact of the world's worst and noisiest drivers I had ever encountered.

Karl's wife, Margaret, dressed in a little white duster, was sitting on the couch looking shiny-clean after her shower. She was very surprised that I had arrived. Their house was much like ours in the States, furnished with some much used furniture, compliments of the warehouse of TWA.

They immediately asked me if I'd like to go to a party. I was exhausted after that long trip that began early that morning in Paris, but still so excited that I couldn't resist the invitation. I said , "I'd love to." A visit from any of the American folks or friends is a rarity. They seemed anxious for me to meet their friends.

Margaret didn't even change clothes. Leaving all the electric lights on and the doors open, we went out the door, down the sandy road and into a small house. It was like going into a nightclub. The smoky, smelly, noisy house belonged to a bachelor called J.J. "He's been married and divorced three times," Margaret whispered to me. Even though this was Wednesday night, it was like our Friday back home. Confusing as it seemed, I found that the Moslem Holy Day is on Friday, so Thursdays and Fridays are their weekend days. Everyone goes back to school and work on Saturday, just as we do on Monday. My sleepy jet-lagged head had to figure this one out later. It was only one of many turnarounds I had to get used to in this land on the other side of the world.

J.J. was homely and clownish. With an all-encompassing gesture, he extended his arm and explained that I could play poker as some people were doing, dance to the loud music as others were, or eat the pizza that one lady was taking out of the oven this very minute. I was dazed by this unexpected party.

"I thought liquor was banned over here," I blurted out.

"That's why I have to hold a bootlegger's party here in my house," J.J. explained. He offered me the home brew. "You have a choice of this kind which we call 'brown sidiki'

6

or 'white sidiki', "he said. It's not like you get back in the States, but when it's all you can get, it even tastes good after awhile." I laughed and said anything would do. Karl and Margaret were introducing me to everyone-about 15 people in all. I felt like I was sleepwalking.

I joined the card players for a few hands, but about 1:30 I interrupted Karl long enough to say I had to get some sleep but could find my way by myself, as Margaret had shown me the room I was to sleep in. It was two-year-old Leila's nursery where they had put up a borrowed bed for me, having moved Leila into a back room.

I excused myself, not feeling one bit missed in that noisy, smoky place. I walked outside into the moonlit Arabian night, marveling that I didn't even need a sweater in February in the middle of the night. The walled-in houses on the compound looked forbidding and all alike. I found myself outside J.J.'s wall, not knowing which direction to go. The narrow little sandy street went in four directions, past cement walls. Much as I hated to, I had to return to the house and ask someone to direct me. I felt as though I would get lost in that maze and never find my way.

The front door was slightly ajar when I got back to their house, only two walls away. Their lights were all on full blast and the air conditioning was buzzing away. I later found out that all their utilities were free and they always left their doors open. There were strange catlike howls coming from the yards and I found that stray cats adopted families and just stayed in their yards to eat the garbage thrown out of the back door. No one ever petted the dogs or cats which were sickly looking and unloved, but they still hung around the walls. It seemed weird, but I couldn't think anymore about it tonight--it just seemed "unreal" was my last thought as I fell into bed, exhausted. Hard to believe that I had come all the way from Paris just yesterday morning, not even twenty four hours ago. My last thought as I was swept into a night of fantasies and mixed up dreams connected with the eternal whirring of the air-conditioning unit in the windowless bedroom, was that I could hardly believe this was happening to me. Again I thought that Aladdin and his magic lamp had nothing on me!

CHAPTER II

EVE BURIED HERE, OTHER SURPRISES TEST MY CREDULOUSNESS

I was in a semi-sleep all night and it took awhile to orient myself when I heard whispery little voices in the hallway.

"All I can see is that she's got furry white slippers," I heard.

"What does she look like?" another voice asked.

"I've forgotten," the first voice said.

Opening my eyes I found it was dark in the windowless room and I wondered if it was dawn. The air-conditioner droned on and I knew that I had heard it subconsciously all night.

"Hello," I called to the unseen persons in the hall. It was Terry Clare who answered as she and her little friend skipped into the room. "Hi Aunt Claire," this unbelievably cute little six-year-old said, smiling and dimpling. Her friend skipped over to the bed and repeated, "Hi Aunt Claire", and immediately adopted me, as did all Terry's friends after awhile.

Putting my peignoir on over my shorty nighty, I walked through the hallway, past the bathroom and into the kitchen where Margaret was making coffee, toast and scrambled eggs. "Sure smells good," I said. Sitting at the oblong table in the 14 x 14 foot kitchen were blonde eight-year-old Julie and the baby, Leila, with her dark hair and deep set blue eyes. Leila was born right here in Jiddah two years ago. Margaret said that immediately after her birth, she was told to decide whether the child would be an Arabian citizen or American -- no dual citizenship. Margaret said "American". Leila didn't smile, she just watched me curiously.

We were all so excited that I was actually here in Arabia that it was only at this moment that the reality actually hit home. Tall Karl, i.e. the "big K", walked in the door at this moment. I questioned why he wasn't at work. He explained again that in the Moslem world Thursday and Friday are their weekends, therefore all business and schools are closed on those two days. I had a lot to learn. This third world seemed topsy turvy in relation to our way of life.

Close behind Karl, another young man walked through the door and I was introduced to their good friend, Jan, who, I found, played a constant and continuing role in the daily life of this family. As Margaret introduced me to this nice looking young man who appeared to be in his thirties, she said that like Karl, he taught English to the Saudi airline employees. Upon Margaret's request, he promised to bring his under-the-sea slides one evening to show me what the underwater world beneath the legendary Red Sea was like, as he was also an avid scubadiver.

"I just came in from diving," he said. I was totally impressed that he had been down in the fabulous Sea that had opened for Moses and his followers and was the scene of many historic happenings in the Bible.

Now it seemed as if the house was full of people. A rather normal sized house of two-and-a-half bedrooms, large living room and kitchen, it resembled our small bungalow back home on the inside. Some major differences were: windows were left wide open, flies abounded everywhere and stray cats sat outside waiting for garbage to be thrown out, so they could eat. These strays adopted yards and stayed there, never to enter the house. Each house was walled in by a concrete wall, so the cats made their homes on top of the wall. Mangy looking creatures, I thought.

Margaret then informed Jan that my luggage had been lost enroute. "It was lost between Duluth and Chicago on the first lap of my journey," I said laughingly, but didn't really think it was funny. I envisioned a month without a change of clothes in this place where there didn't appear to be department stores, nor did I have the finances to shop.

"I have a box of clothes from my late aunt in California," Jan said, "you are welcome to them." I thanked him, but wondered how her size could possibly fit me.

He disappeared as quickly as he had arrived and within a few minutes he reappeared leaving a whole box of clothes inside the door. I took them in the bedroom and checked through the box. They may have been wonderful for the right person, but besides being a bit tight on me, they were much too exotic. For instance, one outfit was made of a material resembling spun gold. It also had butterfly sleeves and bell bottom trousers. The exotic clothes made me curious about this aunt, even though I couldn't wear one thing. Fortunately, and to my great surprise, my huge suitcase did arrive in two days. A car delivered it to Karl at work. How they found me, I'll never know, in this land where telephones were scarce and houses and streets had no numbers or names.

Breakfast was over, it was noon, and in walked another of Karl's co-workers, Tom Godfrey. Somehow we all squeezed into big K's car and I prepared myself for my first glimpse of Jiddah..

As we started out, I became aware that there were many continually honking beeps from a whole army of cars. We could hear them from a long distance away. Karl said that the Saudis thought honking was the thing to do. "They have no basic ground rules," he explained, "so they are like kids who just got their first trucks for Christmas and don't know what to do with them."

Of course I believed Karl when he told me, but I never suspected the awful truth of the situation. I had been in Paris a couple of days waiting for my flight to Arabia and I thought Karl must mean the Saudis drive like Parisians, which to my mind was the worst I could imagine. There I nearly suffered a heart attack many times at the screeching and squealing of brakes. But, believe me, this first day in Arabia was a real eye-opener as to what kind of chaos can really be created by a people who have had no prior knowledge of the machine. I found they are literally a people who have tried to close the enormous gap from the camel to our present day technicalities in a few short years. Riding with Karl in Jiddah that first day when I wanted so badly to see the City was practically earth shaking. No wonder Karl swore he had to drive offensively; the screeching of brakes, shouting and swearing in Arabic, accompanied by venomously shaking fists and the most flagrant disregard for the other fellow's rights was a common sight. I say "fellow" because it's against the law for women to drive. We got into a situation where a car pulled right out of a side street in front of us and headed the wrong way down the street, coming at us head-on. As we came nose to nose with his car, the driver flew out of his door, raised his arm shaking a mean-looking fist and began to shout and swear. His eyes had a murderous glint in them. He refused to move. But Karl couldn't and wouldn't move either. The confrontation! By this time the other driver had a whole string of cars behind him, the others having blindly followed the lead car. I was terrified, thinking Karl was going to get himself killed for not doing what those huge Arabs wanted. Karl valiantly held his ground, just as angry as the other driver and his cohorts, who had lined up beside him. Finally, the irate driver, who was completely in the wrong, gave up and started to back up, while the whole army of cars behind him also had to back up. What a mess! In the movies, it would have been hilarious, but this was real and almost like one's life was at stake.

Woven into this endless stream of traffic I saw many things that contrasted with life as we know it in the U.S.A. It was the ancient versus the modern on the King Abdul Aziz Highway leading into the center of Jiddah. Hundreds of white-robed men paraded down the sidewalk in their long white thobes and their square-shaped headdress called a ghutra, sometimes held on by a couple of rings or a black cord called an agal. These distinguished the Sheiks (Shakes) from the common man, I was told. They had piercing brown eyes and were generally virile and handsome, and many of the men were holding hands as they strolled along.

Occasionally, but not often, we caught sight of two or three little black figures, women covered from head to toe, scurrying along the street, clutching their capes and veils closer around them when they observed us looking at them. I marveled at these antiquated customs still surviving in this day of jets and women's liberation. No liberation here. That

ARAB WOMEN
ALIGHTING FROM
A TAXI

OLD MAN ON DONKEY ALONG BUSY CITY STREET

GOATS GRAZING ON GARBAGE IN CITY OF JIDDAH

MASQUE IN
OLD JIDDAH

was one reason no magazines or newspapers were allowed into the country, so as not to corrupt their people from the ancient ways and religious rules of Islam. The Koran, the Moslem's Holy Book, says no man can look upon a woman's face unless he is her father, brother, or husband. Here in Jiddah, often known as the "Bride of the Red Sea", there were some one-story houses built of cement blocks from nearby quarries, but mostly the City was made up of huge villas, all behind massive cement walls.

"The King has thousands of relatives," Karl said, "they are all considered members of the royal family; therefore the King supports them all. Most of the relatives live here in Jiddah and the huge villas have a section to house a man's harem."

"A real harem?" I asked, having only read about such things in fairy tales. "How many wives can one man have?" I laughed in disbelief.

Karl's answer was serious. "According to the Koran, he's allowed to have four wives, but not too many men have four anymore because a husband is required to treat each wife exactly the same and to have no favorites, which would be pretty hard to do, you must admit." Karl chuckled, as he glanced away from his driving. He had such a nice smile and was well known for his delicious sense of humor. "A harem consists of wife/wives, children (of which there are often many), mothers, mothers-in-law, maids, aunts or any other women of the household.

"They all live together in a special section of the house?" I queried.

"The Arab man has his own quarters and is free to come and go as he pleases. He calls his wife when he wants her," Tom Godfrey spoke up from the back seat. He had been pretty quiet back there. "I also hear the whole family eats one meal a day together, perhaps in the mid -afternoon."

We passed a little old man astride a donkey plodding alongside the road. Hanging from a yoke, loaded bags dangled on each side of the ass' head. Both the donkey and the man seemed oblivious of the honking, noisy traffic whizzing by. They continued to progress nonchalantly under the green eucalyptus trees, date palms and other exotic trees that lined the boulevard. Periodically, other donkeys pulling carts trudged along in the same manner. Again we found ourselves face to face in another confrontation with an oncoming stream of traffic on the wrong side of the street. Many policemen were on duty on the streets but, as Karl pointed out, they were ineffective because they had no way to back up their authority when it came to traffic. Karl swore back at the angry Arab who jumped out of his car in a rage, eyes blazing, uttering terrible oaths in Arabic (I guess they were terrible anyway). As he shook his head and his fist at the tall Arab, Karl met him eye to eye at his 6'3" level. Karl held his ground. A policeman came along and managed to back the errant fellow up and direct him into his proper lane.

We traveled on. Unperturbed, Karl now pointed out the King's palace, one block square, surrounded by a high wall with many guards protecting it. Guard houses were on every corner and in the middle of the surrounding block. "Don't you dare take out your camera now, "Karl warned tersely. "We'll get a picture from some strategic place later." I nodded. "When the front lights are on at night, the King is in residence. Jiddah isn't the capital of Arabia--Riyadh is --but they say that the King really loves this City and prefers to be here. Riyadh is 600 miles inland.

It seemed strange not to be free to take pictures. That was only one of the freedoms we Americans take for granted. I took some pictures with my little pocket instamatic which I could pull out of my handbag in an instant and snap a scene. But Karl warned me seriously, that reprisals would be taken against me and, more importantly, against him and his family if I were seen taking photos. "I remember one American was seen taking pictures on the streets of Jiddah. The police followed him home, rifled all his slides in his home, destroyed many of them, and was told he was fortunate to get off with only a threat of jail. And their prisons are terrible," he added.

"But why?" I asked, puzzled.

Karl was a very patient person and he explained. "They only want pictures of the nice modern Arabia to go out of the country. They don't want the outside world to see this rubble and garbage. They are very careful about the image that is created."

It was true that old and new buildings stood side by side. Some of the old ones were crumbling into a garbage heap while even the new ones being constructed were very littered with trash. "It's hard to tell if they're going up or coming down," Karl commented dryly. He was so articulate and patient about explaining everything to me. I was so grateful to my younger brother who had traveled so far in this world (literally) mile-wise. From his first teaching experience in Nome, Alaska, to the Cameroons in West Africa, and Turkey. He had been everywhere and yet his humility was wonderful. "This sand," his gesture purportedly encompassed the whole of Arabia because it is a desert-land, "that they make their concrete from, is not good for long lasting buildings. These that are falling down are not necessarily old. The sand just does not hold up when they make their cement--it is too fine."

I was surprised because I thought these disintegrating structures must be ancient, like in Egypt, and were crumbling from age.

We passed little fruit stands along the busy street, but not many other businesses other than an open chicken stand where they roasted chickens to go, and one barber shop. Karl said we should go to the suk (sook) very soon and that would be another new experience for me. I had no idea what the suk was, but I was to find this experience different from anything I had ever known. I didn't realize how marvelous this suk would be, nor how endless its depths; that was still to come. How interesting this far-away country was and how fortunate I was to have my family here to show and explain it to me.

I marveled at the perfect 80 degree weather with its low humidity in this month of February, and smiled secretly as I remembered the cold and snow I had left in Minnesota only a few days ago. Snow at least four feet deep on the level and temperatures of 20 degrees below zero had been the weather I had left behind. This was winter in Arabia. Summer here was reportedly unbearably hot, sometimes up to 130 degrees, when you hardly ventured outside. Mostly everyone remained indoors with the air conditioners blowing full blast. But in the winter, the sun shone every day. It seemed like paradise to me.

Now we passed a long enclosed wall, where a small group of veiled women, wearing brown garments, were peering in through an iron gate at some unknown scene.

"What are they looking at?" I asked.

Karl said, "These pilgrims come to see Eve's grave inside that 300 foot enclosure. They are possibly Moslems from India, still here from Ramadan."

"Ramadan? Eve's grave?"

"Ramadan is the feast of Islam when Moslems come from all over the world to visit Mecca for the most holy time of the Moslem year. Every follower of Mohammed is required to visit Mecca at least once in his lifetime. They all peer inside that iron gate to see Eve's grave."

He had parked the car alongside the curb and we walked up behind the ladies from India. They stepped back to allow us to look inside the iron bars. I saw a large field with nothing extraordinary inside. In a kind of sign language I conversed with the little brown-faced women whose faces were covered to their eyeballs with their light-colored veils, unlike the black-garbed women of Arabia. I told them I was from America. They nodded and conveyed interest with their inquisitive brown eyes. There really was nothing to see at the proverbial grave of Eve.

But while returning to the car, I pressed Karl to give me more details about Eve being buried there.

"Jiddah means grandmother," Karl said, because Eve is grandmother to the whole human race. In the Koran you read about the first race of people who were a giant race. I heard that Adam and Eve were very tall when they were first created, so tall that their heads reached above the clouds. The angels felt sorry for those two lonely clods who seemed not to fit upon the earth and they went to God to make them

16

GROUP OF KARL'S
STUDENTS - EMPLOYEES
OF SAUDI AIRLINES

LEGENDARY BURIAL
PLACE OF EVE (JIDDAH
MEANS GRANDMOTHER)

ALLEE, YEMANESE HOUSEBOY

RODION RETHBONE, LEILA AND KARL WOMBACHER

shorter, so he did, but they were still 300 feet tall. Legend says that after Adam died at Mt. Arafat, which is near Mecca, Eve walked through the Red Sea and finally came to this place. She died here and they needed a huge field for her body because she was 300 feet tall."

"Do they really believe that?" I asked, as we drove away from Eve's purported resting place.

"Sure," Karl answered with a half smile on his face.

Stopping at a post office on a narrow congested street, Karl went in alone, leaving me in the car to watch the passing scene. There was much to observe. I could see the Red Sea at the end of the street, but I was more absorbed in watching the men in their long thobes, strolling down the street holding hands, which was perfectly acceptable here, even customary. I watched little ladies wrapped in black, scurrying into taxi cabs, jabbering to each other behind their veils, plus a variety of foreign people who were still here from the Haj, or holy days. The Haj takes place during Ramadan and concerns the prophet Mohammed. Those who walked past were dressed in an unbelievable variety of wearing apparel. I was especially intrigued by two old men sitting cross-legged in front of a coffee shop (open-aired), smoking a unique kind of pipe on a stand. The two Arab men in native dress took turns inhaling from a long tube that looked like a vacuum cleaner hose.

While I watched, fascinated, Karl climbed back in the little car, his tall frame folding in like a card table. "Those are called hubbly-bubbly pipes," he said. "I have one at home. Inside the stand is a mixture, a variety of things, like charcoal, (no tobacco, it's against their religion) water, apple peels and I don't know what else. It is lit and heated up, then they smoke it through those long stemmed hoses." I had never seen nor heard anything like it.

Karl grinned again as he got into the car. He showed me a slip of paper. On it was written some Arabic numbers. On the line marked name, it said, "Love Claire".

I looked at him not comprehending.

"I sent the telegram home to Minnesota to your family like

you asked me to, to let them know you arrived here safely," he said and then in the way only Karl could laugh, he guffawed aloud reminding me of when he was a kid and how he would laugh at our kitchen table at something that tickled his funny bone. He would go off into gales and gales of laughter until our seven member family was all laughing until tears ran from our eyes. Now he was laughing in that same way and with him I laughed until I cried, not even knowing why. "I told him to sign the telegram, 'Love, Claire' and when they made out this receipt, they did it in the name of 'Love, Claire', never having heard that term before, I guess. He handed me the receipt to keep with my memoirs and we both wiped the tears of laughter from our eyes. Semantics is an appropriate word here.

As we returned to the compound, we let Tom Godfrey off at his friend's house. The traffic was snarled up worse than ever--as crowded as the New Jersey toll way--but totally out of control. I admired Karl's ability to keep his cool in spite of it. He continued to explain as we waited in long lines of honking compact cars, telling me that westerners (anyone who came from west of Arabia) lived in compounds separate from the Arabian population. They were not encouraged to mingle with the natives, except on a professional basis or in a school setting, as when Karl taught them English. But they did acknowledge him when they saw him outside of the classroom.

"Our friend, Chris Speake, is coming for supper tonight," Karl said. "You've heard us speak of Chris and Bill, haven't you?"

I had heard of Chris and Bill, their close friends since Karl and Margaret had first come to Arabia seven years ago. "Bill and their oldest son are in the States right now," Karl said, "so Chris and Careme are home alone, as Chris couldn't get away from her teaching job at this time. She teaches in the American school with Margaret, while Bill teaches Saudi Arabian airline employees as I do."

I looked forward to meeting Chris Speake. Margaret was baking a succulent leg of lamb while we were out sightseeing and had prepared a gourmet's delight dinner.

Chris and Margaret were in deep conversation when we arrived, and when I was introduced to her, I was surprised at the quiet-voiced, brown-haired, slightly built young woman with whom I shook hands . And to add to my astonishment, her child Careme was a tousle-haired four-year-old boy, not a girl as I had envisioned. Careme sounded like Corrine to me and how was I to know these mideastern names?

Soon Jan arrived and the adults sat down to eat at the kitchen table. It was a wonderful supper, accompanied by spicy conversation and equally spicy curried lamb which almost burned the very tongue out of me. I couldn't eat very much of it, even to be polite.

The children were entrenched in front of the black and white TV watching the only hour of television of the day in English that featured old American cartoons. The other few hours of the television day were dedicated to featuring the King and other notables walking on and off planes and in and out of meetings, but there was no news of what was happening. No news at all. The television audience had little knowledge of what their king was really doing.

Later, the house boy came in to do the dishes and straighten up the house. Julie and Terry had gone with Karl across the street to the compound's small arena to view their once-a-week movie and Margaret and I settled in the living room for a nice long chat. Little Leila only called once from the bedroom. Then we talked about everything. I had arrived only twenty four hours earlier, but it seemed longer than that. So much had happened.

When I finally turned in, I slept around the clock. The jet lag had finally caught up with me-------.

CHAPTER III

JIDDAH, POTPOURRI OF DULUTH'S JENO'S PIZZA, HAREMS, RED SEA AND GARBAGE EATING GOATS

On Friday I found out what jet lag really meant, having slept through the night and the next day, When I woke up, looked at my watch and saw it was 5:30, I wondered whether it was day or night--I had never felt slept out at 5:30 a.m. The aroma of cooking from the kitchen didn't smell like breakfast. I caught sight of a little blonde head peeking around the corner and called to whomever it was. This time it was eight-year-old Julie, the eldest of the three daughters. She was cute, pudgy and wore little round glasses over very blue eyes. I found, as time went on, that Julie was always full of questions and usually chewing on something, whether it was her finger or whatever else there was to chew on.

"Aunt Claire, how come you slept all day?" she asked.

"I slept all day?" I asked, sitting up in bed, astonished at the assumption. When you don't have a window in the room, day or night can slip by very easily. As I went into the kitchen, I found the family was ready to sit down to supper. I couldn't believe I had slept so long. It did clear away the cobwebby feeling I had since my arrival. My jet lag was mostly over.

Karl, Julie and Leila were going to the market. "Do you want to go along?" Karl asked.

"Sure," I said, anxious to see or experience anything new about this foreign land. What would the market be like?

We drove several miles until we arrived at the Jiddah Super Market, a grocery store resembling a small home-owned store at home. In fact, it was geared to the American consumer. Inside I was amazed to find that many foods made in America could be bought here, much of it frozen and very expensive, nevertheless available.

"They even carry Jeno's Pizza," I said to Karl. "How much is this in American money?" I asked not familiar with counting riyals, the exchange at this time being 4.5 riyals to one American dollar. Karl said they were about $4.00 American money. I knew they cost $.99 back in Duluth, their place of origin, but considering the distance it had been shipped, it might be a fair market price.

On our return trip, we passed the King's palace, noting the watchful guards at the gates and corners of the square block walled-in palace, their guns very much in evidence. One block here is equal to three of ours, although it was hard to tell at a glance.

"Besides this palace and his main palace in Arabia's capital city of Riyadh, the King also has a summer place in Taif on top of the mountain," Karl said.

"Taw eef?" I questioned. "How do you spell that?"

He spelled it out for me and said, "Hopefully, we'll find a day to go there".

I hoped we would, too, but at this moment I was wrapped up in the experience of just being HERE. Leila was sitting on my lap, still looking at me soberly, as if she had never seen a stranger before. We got back in time to have turkey soup and hamburgers. "Just like home,". I said. Just as we finished eating, Allee, the Yemenese house boy arrived and immediately started boiling kettles of water, timing them for 20 minutes.

"Don't you dare take a drink from the faucet", Margaret warned me, "we have to boil all our water or you'll get dysentery, really sick". She also had oranges, apples and lettuce soaking in Hilex and Tide detergent. Allee then spent a lot of time scrubbing, rinsing and drying each one. "We have to do this with all fruits and vegetables," Margaret explained, "because of the kind of manure in the soil." She didn't elaborate any further, but later I heard that human manure was used for fertilizer. Our digestive systems were not adapted to this. These were just a few of the precautionary measures necessary to physical survival in Arabia. Also, it was unbelievable to me that women were almost completely restricted outside their homes from what we take for granted as a human right. Western women living in or visiting Jiddah were given a little more leeway than the black-garbed and veiled Saudi women, but I found we couldn't ride in a taxi alone, weren't allowed to drive a car, couldn't appear on the street with shorts on, or any garment that came above the knee. To be safe from being confronted by the police we were cautioned to wear a long dress or "very nice" slacks.

I now also learned there was absolutely nothing in the way of entertainment in the City of Jiddah. No nightclubs or bars of course, because liquor is against their religion, which is synonymous with the law. Westerners had to provide their own recreation within the framework of their compounds. After many years, a group of them had succeeded in importing movies. The men took turns running the films in the evening; one night a week for the family, one for adults and one for children. This was very beneficial in an otherwise desolate encampment when the nights flowed one into another without diversion. In other countries, especially America we have become so ensnared by TV that when we are suddenly confronted with our own inner resources it's quite a culture shock. At least it was to me. I took an "across the world" look at life back home and suddenly realized what a choice Karl and Margaret and all the other Americans had made to be here in Arabia. I wondered all through the month what advantages had kept them here over eight years. I would try to figure that out as time went on.

On the wall of their living room, the Wombachers had a map. Now, for the first time, I looked at Jiddah in respect to the rest of the world. It was a long way from mid-America, I realized, and the largest city on the Arabian side of the Red Sea. Across the sea was Egypt. Jiddah may share in the profits of the oil exported from Arabia, but it was not physically involved, as were the oil rich cities across the country to the east. Arabia takes up three quarters of the Arabian peninsula. The cities built by Aramco and others are modern compared to ancient Jiddah where the population is anyone's guess, as they have no way to take a census. There are no taxes, so there is no way to gauge the population. Estimates of the whole peninsula range from 5 to 6 million people.

Karl startled me as I was looking at the map by coming silently up behind me. He pointed out the vastness of the southern Arabian desert called Rub al-Khali or the "Empty Quarter". "It is estimated to be 250,000 square miles of desert," he said, "They say there are sand dunes 12 miles long and 600 feet high. Even the Bedouins don't venture too far into that mysterious piece of land. Can you imagine anything that vast and empty?" Karl asked, awe in his voice. I could only shake my head in wonderment, trying to figure it out. I couldn't envision it.

"Would you like to meet Rodion? Karl asked

"Rodion Rathbone?" I asked, realizing that he was Basil Rathbone's son. Basil Rathbone played Sherlock Holmes in the movies. "He's your good friend, isn't he?"

Karl nodded, "Yes, both he and Carolyn are our good friends. She is in the States right now. They keep a New York apartment available all the time, but Rodion is here. We'll go see him tonight."

Margaret couldn't accompany us as she was getting the kids ready for bed. "Be sure to invite him for dinner tomorrow evening, "she said as we went out the door and into the dusk of the evening.

I don't know how far it was, or how we got to the villa where Rodion lived, because the streets were so filled with honking cars. A map of the City is as precious as a gold mine, because they just don't exist. But through some traffic, turns and twists, Karl finally stopped in front of a large walled-in villa. We got out of the car, walked through the iron gate and up many brightly lit steps. "This place once belonged to a wealthy Arab family, a sheik with a harem, but was now rented out as apartments," Karl explained. Rodion and Caroline were an exception to the rule that all "Westerners" live on a compound. Rodion was British which may or may not have made a difference.

Karl knocked on the door on the second floor above the wide marble stairway and we waited quite awhile until eventually we heard footsteps. The door opened while I waited breathlessly to see what this son of a famous movie star was like.

A tall, spare man wearing glasses stood in the doorway, looking not at all like I had pictured him. He greeted Karl warmly. So this was Basil Rathbone's son--older than I expected, maybe in his late fifties. He was better looking than his father, his eyes warm, brown and kind behind those glasses. I had heard about him for many years. I couldn't see any resemblance at all to the man in the movies with the cold eyes, hawk-like nose and cold manner.

Rodion turned to me as Karl introduced us, shook hands warmly and invited us in. A long, wide hallway resembled an art gallery, lined with paintings. Rodion led us down the hall past a couple of closed rooms and then turned left into an enormous living room. A Siamese cat jumped at us viciously. I shrieked. Rodion calmly picked it up and deposited it in another room.

"Do you want a drink?" he called from somewhere. Karl said, "Sure". It gave me time to look around. Four couches and several stuffed chairs were placed randomly around the room and the walls were filled with beautiful paintings. They looked like the Masters.

"Rodion painted these," Karl said. "He paints from famous pictures."

They were good! I looked more closely as we removed books and sundry other things from the chairs so we could sit down. Soon Rodion returned, diminished by the hugeness of the room, carrying three glasses filled with pink colored mixed drinks. I commented about his paintings. He said, "I just copy some of the Masters or my favorite artists. They really aren't very good. That one is a copy of Goya and that is one of Van Gogh's that I copied.

"This drink is delicious," I said. "What is it?"

"It's made from sidiki." By now I knew sidiki was the name of the illegal bootlegged liquor made by a Westerner whose name was closely guarded. I learned that his family lived in mortal fear of detection because if caught, he would surely be, at the least, expelled from Arabia, maybe jailed, maybe worse for such a terrible offense against the laws of Islam. It was a well kept secret, though, and while the young man prospered from his lucrative operation, the Americans lived like kings with their cupboards overflowing with "white" or "brown" sidiki.

"I have a special recipe made from a bottle of fruit concentrates, lemon concentrate, sidiki and water," Rodion confided when I expressed an interest in the ingredients that made the 180% brew actually enjoyable.

We had a wonderful time with Rodion. He was extremely likable and interesting, sharing some of his interests and hobbies with us, the latest being a sailboat he was building in order to sail on the Red Sea. It was being constructed in the back, walled-in yard of the villa. He promised to show it to me when we came again in the daylight.

"What is your job with Saudi Airlines?" I asked him.

"Right now I teach pilots to fly," he said. "I was a navigator for TWA for many years, but I got weary of the constant traveling." So he, like the Americans, worked for the Saudi Airlines through TWA.

"That has got to be the biggest pillow I've ever seen," I exclaimed, looking at the fuzzy pillow on the floor, a ten foot long and six foot wide monstrosity. Rodion laughed, "Yes, my son, Rodion, brought it from somewhere at one time. He's at M.I.T. (Massachusetts Institute of Technology) right now."

"When is Caroline coming home?" Karl asked.

"I'm expecting her most any day, You know how that is. You really don't know until someone gets here."

I listened and began to understand the "Malesh" philosophy that ran through the structure of life in this strange land. One says "malesh" and shrugs his shoulders, meaning "Nothing matters, really--there's always tomorrow--or eternity". Each day I was to find more and more the importance of acquiring this all-important attitude in this far-off land of antiquity and mystery, sun and desert. And Rodion was expressing it with a shrug of his shoulders, almost a weary shrug which told me more than he intended. Karl had told many times of Caroline's long trips to the

States where she stayed in their luxurious New York apartment and socialized with some very famous people, both in the theatrical world and in society. But Rodion shied away from all of that. He wanted nothing to do with any of it; hence he stayed on his job in Jiddah, near the world's oldest grave, that of Eve. Rodion apparently relished this kind of living, in this place that stretched back into the antiquities of time. No wonder "malesh" is the slogan of life here. I was still to learn more later.

Karl looked at his watch now. "Oh boy, we'd better get going," he said. "We've been gone too long--it's 10:30 already." Rodion immediately led us down the long, long hallway and gladly accepted the invitation to dinner the next evening. As we passed the masterpieces he and Caroline had collected, we stopped in front of each painting while he explained them to us and told why he loved each one. His favorites were passionately explosive-- El Greco, Mantanya (Gethsemane), Goya and Van Gogh. What a fascinating half hour while I saw another side of Rodion's outwardly quiet nature. His choices reflected a passionate nature.

Out into the balmy Arabian night Karl and I went then. The stars were numerous and low, the air warm and luscious, the night sounds mysterious. Some of the roads were merely sandy alleys and I shivered as a white robed figure walking along the walls suddenly disappeared inside a gate without a sound. There were flickering lights and many stands and stores open. The streets in the main districts were filled with white robed men, their heads wound with their colorful ghutras. The lack of even one woman walking on the street made a strong statement. It was all terribly exciting and the day/night was not over yet. When we got back to the compound, which was about five miles from the main district, we found Margaret wasn't home, but out visiting somewhere. Shortly after, Jan came by, asking if I wanted to see his movies of scuba diving in the Red Sea. "Oh yes," I said enthusiastically, So he left and returned shortly with his projector and movies. We watched the "Underseas Adventures of Jan Copeland". I've never seen such an array of exotic colors and beautiful fish.

Barracuda, sting rays, puffers, moorish delights and more, plus the beautiful coral reefs. I hadn't known that these coral reefs could be very deadly to man.

Jan said he had been scuba diving for four years. In fact, Karl was now one of Jan's students and was also in the movie. Karl's place was within two blocks of the airport. There were jets screaming across the sky day and night. As Jan talked, he often needed to wait for the noise to subside before he could finish his sentence. I couldn't help but mention how overwhelming to me were the contrasts of the old--into antiquity, and the new--into the jet age.

Following the movies, which were surprisingly professional and as interesting as Jacques Cousteau himself, I thanked Jan, as Margaret appeared in the doorway. We ended the evening with some sidiki and good talk.

Later, a far away station somewhere in the world was beaming in an old tune on the B.B.C (British Broadcasting Corporation) that I had learned in my youth, "We Just Couldn't Say Good night". A good theme song for night people like Karl and me. Margaret had turned in earlier, Karl had finished his nightly shower and was going to bed. He was almost more of a night owl than I. But it was 2 a.m. and I was about to fly into the arms of Morpheus myself. What would tomorrow bring?

CHAPTER IV

ARABIAN SUK (MARKET) SHROUDED IN MYSTERY, INTRIGUE--GENIE WELL AND ALIVE

Pure luxury, I thought, as I lay in the hot noonday sun beside the tranquil swimming pool. This was pure heaven. The rectangular 50 foot pool was deserted, the sky clear and blue. A welcome breeze billowed the aquamarine colored water. The pool was walled in like every building in Jiddah and completely private. The only movement that disturbed the complete silence of the afternoon was that of a small dark man from the adjacent country of Yemen who cleaned this place, minding his own business, never even casting a glance in my direction. I basked in the wonder of it all.

My breath caught in my throat as the reality sent waves of excitement pulsating through my entire body--this is real--I am here --it is no dream. My problems were far across the ocean, a couple of oceans, plus the Red Sea. But, an anxiety returned to plague me. I had no way of knowing what was going on back in Proctor, Minnesota, U.S.A., absolutely no way of being in touch. I couldn't let myself dwell on it; I chose to succumb to the midday warmth, turning over in the bright sun, accepting the alternative to enjoy this siesta time along with the natives in the mideast who use the early afternoon to rest. I must think of the here and now. It wouldn't help to worry about my son who I had reluctantly left with my husband.

Later Margaret and I took one of the thousand taxis to the suk, a hair-raising experience in itself. The taxi driver, like all the other drivers, drove like a maniac and, like the others, honked his high little horn continually. I was sure we were about to collide with some other car. My heart was leaping like a gazelle all the time, but we finally got there safely. Karl and I had walked through a small part of that most interesting market place last night. The sights I saw were unreal to me.

28

Last night Karl and I had gotten out of his car at a modern building, the Queen's building, so named because she had been instrumental in its design. It was 17 stories high, towering above everything else in Jiddah. We took the elevator to the top of it where we could view the City. A gorgeous sunset over the Red Sea made me long to be an artist to capture its beauty. The derelict ships, listing heavily against the sunset were like a fairy tale. I watched in wonder at the Moslem men running to their nearest mosque to pray, as the Muezzin called them in a tuneless voice. Karl said their music was based on a quarter note instead of a half note like ours and so grated on our ears accustomed as we are to our type of music. "This is their fifth time of prayer today and their last," Karl explained, as we saw them all kneeling in unison, bowing toward Mecca as they chanted their prayer in unison.

Today, as Margaret and I had stepped from the taxi at the Queen's building, I noticed the terrible contrast of the beautiful modern building, next the crumbling ruins, cement bricks scattered everywhere amid much rubbish. But, now we walked into the magic streets of the suk where we were translocated into another world. Some of the many intricate winding streets were brightly lit and the displays of the merchant's goods were colorful and modern. We saw many men dressed in their long white garments called thobes (tobes), bandanas wound around their heads, little black veiled women, an occasional donkey cart and narrow cobblestone streets. Margaret told me you could find almost any commodity you desired somewhere in this crazy octopus-like quarter called the suk. It was enchanting.

What fascinated me most was that, like the City itself, this suk seemed to be an uncharted world. In a few minutes after entering the maze, I found myself unbelievably lost. The more I twisted and turned on different little paths and streets, the more befuddled I became. At one time I wandered away from Margaret and found that I had been truly fortunate to have hired one of the small dark-eyed basket boys who beg you to hire them to follow you around and carry your packages. These young fellows from eight to fifteen years old are around at every turn of the maze. They sometimes speak limited English, are great little advisors, even helped bargain with the shrewd shopkeepers when I purchased an item. Every item was open to negotiation, akin to buying real estate back home. We offered a low price and the shopkeeper came back with a high bid, and the game of high-low became a compromise somewhere in between.

We came to the "street of gold", not really a street, but a narrow walkway where the lights flashed brightly on case after case of gold bracelets, rings and necklaces, silver and pearl. We paused at the shops in one street where the most lovely materials were displayed. Fabrics like we have never seen nor dreamed of--every kind of fabric and color.

A smiley, talkative Arab named Mohammed, wearing the traditional ghutra on his head, overflowing with charm, ran a news shop. When Margaret introduced me to him , he immediately asked about my mother, whom he remembered from her visit to Arabia the year before. We bought postcards and a book in English about Arabia. It was fortunate that I bought that book when I did, as I never did see another one written in English while I was there. The small stand was well stocked with newspapers and magazines, but no others in English. As we left the open stand, Margaret explained that the only English newspaper available here was the International Herald Tribune which originated in Paris, came through Beirut and then into Arabia. A paperboy delivered it to their house, Margaret said, but it was two days late and often censored. Some articles would be scissored out or blacked out with black crayon.

I was wide-eyed at this strange world in which my brother and his family had lived for eight years. "You hardly have any contact from the outside world at all, do you Margaret?" I asked.

My small, 5'1" sister-in-law, with her boyish haircut and olive skin burned almost native brown by the sun, said in her definite voice, "I suppose that's true, but we hardly think of it anymore. We can hear Voice of America late at night,

ANOTHER FAMOUS
MOSQUE IN CITY
ON RED SEA

MINISTRY
OF FOREIGN
AFFAIRS BUILDING

MATERIAL SHOPS IN SUK (SOOK)

SMILING MERCHANT, MOHAMMED, WHO
SOLD BOOKS AND POSTCARDS

about 2 a.m. or the BBC; and we subscribe to Newsweek, which eventually gets here two weeks late and is often censored, but---" and her voice trailed off as she seemed to try to think of some other avenues or links with the outside world. They were apparently nil. She shrugged her thin little shoulders and smiled her wide grin in her very tanned face which made her lovely teeth appear to gleam twice as white as they were. She spread her hands palms up and said, "Malesh." That was a very expressive remark used often in conversation here.

We passed a street where many booths of fruit, large, giant sized luscious apples, oranges, bananas and dates were piled high in a dazzling array of prosperity. The perfection was spoiled by billions of little black flies buzzing and landing on these tempting fruits, Mother Nature's paradise-creations. Flies were everywhere in Jiddah, a fact which I had to learn to ignore and accept because there was nothing I nor anyone else could do about it.

I noticed we were very deep into the suk; it was like being in a cavern where, the deeper we went, the darker and more antiquated it became. I felt a bit frightened. After walking through the brightly lit streets, we were now in a very dark area where the figures of those huge, bearded Arabs were almost terrifying in the shadows of their unlit booths.

"Come on," Margaret urged, I want to show you this place run by the cave man." We now stepped into a dark cavern-like place where a shaggy, dirty and toothless old man sat humped-up in a corner. You almost couldn't see his wares, it was so dark in there. He had second hand and antique-type things. When it was antique or second hand in Arabia, believe me, it might stem from the unknown ages of eternity. Some things were broken. This experience was frightening because the shrewed old cave man must have hated westerners--or maybe himself. He was grumpy and mean, could bargain only in broken English, but wanted the highest prices for even his broken-down merchandise. Many things were broken, not good for anything. He was adamant in his bargaining and the place was so filthy and dark that I wouldn't have been surprised to see Aladdin's genie appear out of a dusty corner. Meanwhile, Margaret was whispering that many of these things some silver jewelry for instance, broken and tarnished, had actually been hand crafted by the Bedouins in the desert. We would have bought, except that the surly Arabian wouldn't bargain and kept shaking his shaggy old head at our offers for his merchandise, even crummy and broken as it was. We refused to pay. Just then the Muezzin was chanting his call from the balcony at the top of a distant minaret, near the steeple of a mosque. All the surrounding shops were quickly being closed as their owners ran to pray. Margaret said that he calls, "God is great," four times plus other phrases ending with "Prayer is better than sleep". Only the cave man continued to smoke his hubbly-bubbly, that gigantic pipe sitting on a stand. He didn't budge himself when the call for prayer came. We got out of there, however. I was grateful that Margaret found her way out because almost every place was closed down and it was very scary. Then we were back up in a higher part of the suk, out onto King Abdul Azziz Street where we hailed a cab to go home.

CHAPTER V

RODION RATHBONE--SON OF BASIL

No opportunity to write yesterday, but much has happened. Overly tired Friday night, I crawled into bed at 3 a.m., but didn't sleep all night. I got up with Karl, Julie and Terry early and cooked breakfast for them while Margaret slept in. She hadn't been feeling well.

Later she and I took one of the many taxis and went to the market, which catered to Americans. Most of the food was frozen, but almost everything seemed to be available. No pork, of course, on account of Moslem law and religion, whose laws are the same. The King rules the country of Arabia with an iron hand, in exact accordance with the Koran, the "Bible" of Islam.

Open booths along the way were loaded with delicious fruits and vegetables, mostly brought in from Lebanon, that place with the perfect climate. Other food had come in on the ships from many countries, especially the U.S. and Holland as well as others. Brand names I recognized from home were 7-Up, Pepsi Cola, Kraft Cheese, Tortinos and Jeno's pizza.

Most everyone had returned to school, Karl and Margaret as teachers of English, Julie and Terry as students. It was Sunday, the first working day of the week for the Arabs.

Rodion Rathbone had come for dinner last evening. Because Margaret is a super cook, she outdid herself by serving a leg of lamb, mint jelly, potatoes, gravy and fresh garden beans, along with Karl's homemade apple wine. The food was delicious and the conversation stimulating. Rodion had a quiet manner and seemed a bit aloof because he was a very private person. But his British accent, when he spoke, was wonderful to listen to.

Karl had an appointment at 7:15 to show movies to the Natural History Society with Jan Copeland. (A little Arab or Yemenese house boy walked into my private swimming pool area. He didn't even glance my way while I sat there by the sun- splashed pool, just disappeared somewhere).

While Margaret bathed the kids and put them to bed, Rodion and I sat alone in the front room and talked. He was a warm, delightful man, although very reticent, especially about being the son of the famous Basil Rathbone, movie star. Karl had mentioned more than once that Rodion hardly ever mentioned his famous heritage. If we had not been alone, I might not have ventured the questions I did, but it was Rodion who first brought up his father when I asked him if he had ever gone to college. He said he had first studied electrical engineering, then had gone to California where he met his father for almost the first time in his life. Rodion hesitated a few minutes, (it seemed like an eternity), recrossed his long legs and then began telling me about his life. I listened, spellbound.

"My mother and father were divorced when I was only two years old. Mother then took me back to her home in England where she played in Shakespearean theatre on the stage."

"What was her name?" I asked wondering if I had ever heard of her.

"Marion Foreman," he answered. "I grew up in boarding schools. Of course they were the best." He winced as if it were painful.

"Rodion, pardon me if I'm intruding on your privacy," I said, "but how did you really feel about your famous father during those years? Do you mind?" I asked, hoping I wasn't trodding on hallowed ground when he waited so long to reply.

Then, while gazing into the distance, he finally answered, "I can't even answer that question to myself. My memories of growing up are so mixed up. Sometimes I felt downright bitter because here my dad was a famous movie star, noted especially for his Sherlock Holmes roles, and yet I had never met him. All the other boy's fathers came to visit them, taking them out for a holiday and they cared about their sons. I was in a worse position than being fatherless. I was very lonely, I guess.

My heart went out to Rodion Rathbone, the shy

34

introverted man who had been surrounded by theatre people; his famous father, his well known actress mother and even his wife, Caroline, who still held ownership in a summer stock theatre in Wisconsin. Margaret had told me that when Rodion and Caroline were married in Hollywood, every famous movie star of the day attended. Margaret had once seen the newspaper clippings-- Marlena Dietrick and many more of the beautiful people were in the picture. And yet here he was, Rodion Rathbone, shy and lonely, almost an outcast, a long time resident of Saudi Arabia. Now, I listened intently because he continued. "Later, I toured with my mother while she played theatres all over England. I really had many bad experiences being backstage like I was. Mostly I learned to hate the theatre. Once, while our company was staying in one hotel, we left our room to go to dinner. Suddenly this nasty little Welshman confronted us and accused us of trying to leave without paying our bill. We had money and didn't intend to leave just then, but it left me with a lot of bitterness toward that kind of life." He shuddered.

I could hear Margaret saying good night to the kids now and I hoped she wouldn't come into the living room just then. I was so interested in what he was telling me. We had a real rapport in this unrepeatable moment.

"Suddenly I was fed up with that life, so I wrote to my father." Rodion's marvelous British accent was a wonderment in itself. "To my amazement," he said, sipping his sidiki, "he was ready to embrace me as a son for the first time in my life. You see, to escape from my mother's over-possessiveness, I fled to America--to my father. He acted so happy to see me that I could hardly believe it. This man, this stranger, who had never even acknowledged me before. Can you possibly imagine how I felt?" Rodion leaned forward looking directly into my eyes. He actually cared if I understood or not. I nodded, completely engrossed. "Basil introduced me to all the famous people of Hollywood. I was 21 years old at that time and suddenly I was catapulted from an extremely sheltered life into the middle of Hollywood's social scene. In fact, Basil's wife was the most famous

Hollywood hostess at that time. That was really a shock to me--it all was!" I realized then that Rodion was probably the understater of the year! I couldn't comprehend how to fill in all the in-between lines. He covered it all in two sentences-- the parties, the excitement of Hollywood when actor/actresses were the Kings and Queens reigning supreme in America. I tried to figure what years those were. Most likely the 1930's.

Back to the swimming pool where I was writing. Now the house boy was watching me from inside the clubhouse. Besides, it was time for my appointment with Mia, the Dutch beauty operator.

It was Monday afternoon now, and I was lazing by that wonderful pool again in the sun--luxury unbelievable.. The sun shone eternally with never a cloud in the sky. I came from a land where there was hardly ever a clear blue sky and the Great Lake Superior could turn a beautiful afternoon into a cold, windy nor'easter in the blink of an eye. The flies buzzed -- the quiet was complete, being siesta time. I was alone. I thought of my family back home--it was so very far away and removed. It was nine hours earlier in Proctor, Minnesota - 5 am, difficult to picture it all. They were still sleeping, and would be, for at least two hours more. My world was filled with sand, heat, white robed Arabs and veiled women. Wow! What a different scene! I prayed that they were doing okay without me.

Back to Rodion and our engrossing conversation. He told me an interesting anecdote then about a famous star in Hollywood. "One of the nicest people I met in Hollywood was Marlene Dietrick."

"Really?" I was listening.

"Oh yes," His brown eyes even twinkled for a moment. "She was a little naughty, a real tease. To show you something about how wonderful and down to earth she was, I'll tell you about one time when we visited her daughter, Maria, who lived above Marlene's apartment in the same building. When we went up there to find her, we found Marlene down on the floor scrubbing it for Maria." Rodion smiled secretly. He must have thought that it was wonderful to find the enigmatic, glamorous lady of the movies down on her knees being unglamorously human. We both laughed, appreciatively sharing a special moment. As he lit a cigarette I encountered his warm brown eyes and we really had a treasured moment of rapport.

"I played the part of the playboy for awhile." He quickly hid his feelings and jumped back into a more comfortable narrative of his life. "It was quite a shock to me to be flung into that society. Basil's second marriage was very successful, his wife gave wonderful parties. But, I wasn't prepared for my--Basil--to clasp me to his bosom as he did. I was trying to get away from that. Then the war with Germany started. England was in it at this time, but not America as yet. I tried to join the RAF (Royal Air Force), but they wouldn't pay my way back to England, so I went to Canada and joined the Canadian Air Force. I never did get back to school." He then skipped over the war completely. "Later, I taught at a private girls' school. They were spoiled children. I hated it! Finally I teamed up with TWA as a navigator and, of course, now I teach their pilots how to navigate. I've been with the airlines ever since."

"You've had a very interesting life, haven't you, Rodion?" I asked. "And you're also an artist." The house had become so quiet that I wondered where Margaret had disappeared after putting the three girls to bed. No sound broke the silence. Rodion went into the kitchen and soon returned with one of his delicious drinks concocted from Karl's sidiki. He amazed me by continuing to talk.

We talked about his wife, Caroline. "I don't know if you know it or not, but she owned that outdoor summer stock theatre near Green Bay, Wisconsin, for about 25 years. We traveled there every summer for the productions, so you see I've been on the fringes of the stage ever since I was born," he reiterated.

"I hope she comes back from the States before I leave," I said. He didn't comment. "Have you ever acted, yourself?" I asked him.

He sipped his drink and nodded, smiling. "Surprisingly I did. After I met my father, I was in two films with him.

They're still around by the way, on the late, late movies. One was 'The Tower of London'. I was the one who got my head chopped off in the tower." He gestured deprecatingly and laughed self-consciously. "The name of the other film eludes me at the moment." (I never did find out the name of it). "But, I'd like to tell you something about my father. He was actually quite a warm person in spite of his cold image in the movies. In the second movie when I played a bit part, I was directed to salute my father and say 'I am reporting for duty, sir'. Rodion leaned forward to make a point. "Imagine this veteran movie star who was particularly noted for always knowing his lines, when he could not respond to me. We rehearsed it at least 20 times, but he was so shook, because it was me, his son, standing there before him--that he was immobilized." Rodion laughed and sat back smiling while recalling this peculiar incident in a life where he had never known his father, but now Basil was overcome with the realization of his own paternity.

Later the conversation turned to his equally famous mother in England. "She came to visit us here in Jiddah four years ago," he said. She didn't know that liquor was forbidden in Arabia, and you have to be aware of her long standing habit and belief that she attributes her longevity to drinking a quart of scotch a day to appreciate this."

"Oh no!" I nodded for him to go on, like a child who knew the end of the fairy tale.

"Yes," He nodded his dark head and grinned as he said, "She had two bottles of the best stuff right on top of her clothes in the suitcase." But funny as it sounds now, she almost cried when she saw the customs agent pour the stuff down the drain right in front of her eyes. In her inimitable English voice, she said, 'My good man, that's very good scotch, you know.' The customs people just glared at her and poured it all away."

"What did she do while she was here?" I asked.

Rodion's brown eyes again twinkled behind his glasses. With a wry smile he replied. "I had to go out and find some bootlegged stuff. I really don't drink much liquor myself. This is kind of an exception." He held his glass up.

Margaret came into the room then from wherever she had been and she caught the last few sentences. "Rodion's mother could recite all the parts of all the characters in any Shakespearean play. She would act out the whole play for us."

"Really?" I asked incredulously. "Most of us can't even understand Shakespeare, much less memorize whole plays!"

"Caroline invited us over for supper one night while Rodion's mother was here," Margaret said. "You never would have expected this very aloof lady--she is very large, like almost 300 pounds--to want the kids close to her because she wore very dressy taffeta-silk sort of clothes, but she really liked our girls and paid a lot of attention to them. They took to her, too".

"I used to write to her in the theatrical nursing home she is in," Rodion said. "But when I visited her and asked if she got my letters, she couldn't remember. It seemed to confuse her." He shook his head sadly. "She doesn't know if I come anymore or not."

The evening with Rodion Rathbone was very memorable to me. Even if this meeting had not taken place in Jiddah, Saudi Arabia, I would have found him to be an interesting wonderful human being. But, it was only one of a series of extraordinary days and evenings. I couldn't get over it, Karl and Margaret were surrounded by such interesting friends. I began to understand a little bit about their love of being there.

CHAPTER VI

WHAT ATTRACTS AMERICANS TO THIS FAR OFF ARID LAND?

It's 5 a.m. on Tuesday morning. Karl just went to bed, but he is usually more of a night person than I am. My younger brother comes across to me as a kind and just father (like our own dad), a thoughtful and helpful husband and a wonderful brother. He's a great communicator who loves to share his adventures with others. Fortunately, at present, it's me.

Before I finish Rodion's story, I must tell of Monday's exciting events. Margaret and I took an hour-long trip to the suk this morning, in a taxi that careened perilously through the City. It seems as though one's life depends on the spin of the wheel when riding through that traffic of drivers who pay no attention to laws. Anyway, I saw that you could spend an untold number of days in that marvelous world of the suk without seeing it all or ever getting tired of the variety of commodities it offers--the old and the new.

Then I took an hour's siesta at the pool and went to Mia's for a shampoo and set at noon. It might seem as though this bit of information is hardly worth mentioning until you realize this: a beauty operator in Jiddah runs an illegal business. If they raided her house, the police would likely destroy all the equipment and her two dryers which she went to great lengths to smuggle into the country. Perhaps her family would be deported, or worse. It's against the Moslem religion for women to be "vain" about their looks. They can wear kohl (sounds like coal) to make up their eyes. It is an eye liner, much like mascara. They can wear polish on their fingernails in all colors, rings on every finger and thumb, but that's all the makeup they are legally allowed to use. My beauty treatment cost 15 riyals ($3.50).

Going to Mia's was somewhat of a hassle that day because of all it entailed. Margaret had to taxi across the city to Mia's house the day before, go in and make the appointment. Margaret didn't intend to go with me today, but because the only communication between the Arabian driver and the rider is by pointing your finger in the direction you wish him to go and repeating "alle tu" (a little further this way) until you come to the destination. There are no streets or numbers and no English is spoken by the taxi driver. Margaret had to take Leila in the taxi and then turn around to return home. The taxi ride cost about fifty cents, so the cost was negligible, but time is valuable.

Mia's place was humming with activity. It was the first time I saw the women from different areas of the city get together. Then I found out about news networking. Like magpies, the ladies chattered about who was doing what, who was out of the country and where they were, etc. They all knew about me coming to visit. Five ladies there were friendly. Mia was the coordinator, with a low guttural voice. She spoke with a thick Dutch accent. She was from Holland, she told me, while her expert fingers curled my hair. Mia was short and stocky, with bleached blonde hair and the mideast attitude of "malesh" (Eternity is forever and there's always tomorrow, so why hurry?)

Two hours later when Karl came to pick me up, he complimented me on the transformation Mia had wrought. "Mia's place is an experience in itself," I told him as we climbed in the car, where already the honking horns drowned out my voice.

We drove around the belt line of Jiddah which led along the shore of the Red Sea. I was disappointed that the famous Sea's beauty was marred by litter and garbage piled and scattered in mountainous heaps. The Red Sea isn't red either. I had envisioned it to be blood-red, from the long ago biblical time when the Egyptians were drowned while chasing the break-away Israelite slaves. Today, derelict ships were disintegrating in the Bay, making dramatic silhouettes against a red-black sky at sunset. It looked like a graveyard of ships dying by degrees in a sea of timelessness. The whole atmosphere of this ancient city was one of time immemorial, old as antiquity, stretching backward into forever. The very difference from my own life

41

in small town America was what gave it an enchantment I had never experienced before. I loved being here--but just for a visit.

Monday evening I walked to the end of Karl's gravel street to the open air theatre, where there were rows of chairs set up for the movies, as well as a stage that had been built by volunteers. This night, rehearsals were in full swing for the annual Follies which, I heard, was the highlight of the year for the "Westerners" in Jiddah. Any person who wished could perform, make costumes, teach dancing, create scenery, apply makeup or any one of the other myriad tasks that go into show business.

"This social evening, the only real social occasion of the year, was attended by all the westerners in the city. There were even reservations with friends at certain tables while they enjoyed their sidiki and watched the show. (The bootlegger makes a fortune on this night). I heard that the Saudis stay discreetly away from this gathering.

It was fun to sit in on the rehearsals, there in the dark under the low cap of stars in the cool balmy evening. This year there were 30 acts, many of them of professional quality. I sat in the back, in the perfect night air, alone, and watched them rehearse. It was wonderful.

Two people were setting up scenery because it was a night of dress rehearsals. The choreographer, a tall beautiful dark-haired girl with long sexy legs, was practising with one group of dancers while a middle-aged man sang soulfully out into the dark emptiness of the night. I was astonished at the power of his voice, while he did a perfect imitation of Al Jolson's "Mammy".

Two young couples were next to go on stage, singing "Money, Money, Money". They danced this gay little number in a staccato type rhythm which made me laugh out loud in the dark. It was delightful. I couldn't get over the amount of talent up there on that stage. For a moment I forgot I was in Arabia. They created an illusion that this was a rehearsal hall in Anytown, America. They were so serious about this endeavor. They had worked hard and were visibly excited about this annual "night out" when there were no other "nights out" as we know them back home. Here, beneath the stars, I concluded there were many frustrated hams or dramatists in the group of Americans who choose to live here.

Karl was in a small singing group. Again I realized how he loved music; it was the essence of his life. He had sung with this group at the American Embassy recently. I remembered when he was in kindergarten and Miss Lundeberg told my mom that he was the first pupil in all her many years of teaching who had perfect pitch. He was the director of the little kindergarten band that year and Mom wrote news for our Proctor Journal, so she could give him voice lessons. Karl became the consummate musician at the piano and always sang in choirs and choruses wherever he went.

These people called "westerners" (everyone is west of Saudi Arabia, almost) live on compounds provided by the airlines or other companies; i.e. Raytheon, TWA, Lockheed, etc. Some had lived here as long as twelve years, some less, some longer. I concluded that the Americans were a cross section of America. From every corner of the U.S.A. they came, to spend at least a few years halfway around the world. Why?, I asked myself again. I pondered that big question in the back corner of the dark outdoor theatre on that February evening. I knew it was not as if they were the castoffs of our society. All of them were sharp, good looking, smart, fine people. It was not because they were disillusioned with their country, I reasoned further. They all proclaimed great love and loyalty to their native land. Almost to a person, these Americans would cite the "money" as their reason for living in this far-off lonely, hot desert land.

"I got so tired of cutting the grass every Saturday and doing the same things on Sunday," one young man said. "yet not having enough left out of my paycheck to ever go anyplace. I put my nose to the grindstone, never having anything to show for it, but a broken nose. Now, here, I have money, plus I get airline passes to travel wherever I want to go--one of the perks of working for an airline."

"When we were home, we saved to buy a nice house, but

prices kept skyrocketing until we were unable to save a dime," another young housewife said. "We weren't even able to save the minimum down payment. My husband was a mechanic for the airline. One day he came home and told me about this job posted on the bulletin board for a mechanic in Saudi Arabia. I was working, too, in California, where we live. We couldn't make ends meet. We couldn't resist the temptation to do better, especially when he told me the monthly salary. We thought that in two years we would have the down payment for a home, maybe even better, then we could come back," Becky looked at me with troubled eyes as she said plaintively, "But that was four years ago. Now, if and when we do go back, we don't know if we could settle back into that humdrum life again." Becky lived next door to Karl and Margaret and she had a full-time, live-in African maid, who left her free to devote her time experimenting with new hairdos, and changing make-up, which seem to be Becky's two top priorities, while her husband and children come in a poor third and fourth.

"Prices have skyrocketed back home so much even since we left, jobs are at a premium so we continue to hold tight and stay here year after year," said Becky's very tall, six -foot-four inch good-looking young husband, Clel, joining in our conversation. "We get free housing and utilities, have a lot of nice friends in the same boat as we are and five free passes to go anywhere we wish." He grinned in an appealing way. "We can stand it here," he said.

Somehow, in spite of the perks, it seemed out of character to see Americans accept such a different kind of life for these fringe benefits. I wondered. It's true the Arabians do need the westerners to teach them the English language, as Karl and Jan do, and the technical knowledge of airplane mechanics and electronic skills to teach to their people and inculcate the knowledge of the modern world. The Arabs adamantly refuse to accept foreigners into their society, yet they make good use of these talented foreigners. Very few of our people have been entertained in an Arabian villa, and if they have, it probably wasn't more than once. There is little intercourse between the two societies. Consequently, our people stay on their compounds, socializing with other English-speaking people. Are both societies exclusive by their own choosing? I didn't know. The Christian church wasn't allowed to function there, as I mentioned earlier. Once a month, at the American Embassy, a missionary priest would say the Mass for Catholics and a protestant missionary would hold services on an opposite Sunday. A covert note was passed around, just like the early Christians did when they were about to meet to break Eucharist together. The Christians are considered infidels in this society.

I have summarized the drawbacks I might suffer if I were a resident in Saudi Arabia, such as boiling the drinking water from the faucet for 20 minutes before drinking it to avoid dysentery. I come from the region of the great fresh water lake, Lake Superior, where we are spoiled insofar as we have an unlimited supply of wonderful cold, fresh water. Although Karl was from the same small town, adjacent to the city of Duluth, Minnesota, he was now accustomed to the inconvenience. You can't bring magazines or newspapers into the country and there are few newspapers or magazines inside of Arabia, in English. This censorship would be terrible for my "free thinking soul" to swallow. The temperature is well over 100 most of the year (I was here during the winter months when it was a perfect 75-80 degrees) and one must stay inside with the air-conditioning much of the time. I was happy with that present perfect weather, having come from one of the coldest states in the Union. Because we have unseasonable weather much of the year, I have been conditioned to staying indoors to keep warm when it's cold, or bundling up with pile-lined coats, gloves, and warm headgear. I guess it's a matter of posture. There is absolutely no culture or night life for Americans in this city, although there appears to be much socializing among the Arabians. The "westerners" have a club where they pay dues which go for the imported American movies shown on the compound three times a week, even though most of the pictures were quite old. This was a recent innovation and it enriched their lives considerably. Also there was that hour a day when old American TV programs were shown such as: Mr. Ed (a real oldie starring a talking horse), episodes of the Partridge family and Family Affair (about a man taking care of his niece and nephew). Some of the programs shown on the TV were at least 20 years old. The kids ate it up. Otherwise TV consisted of long drawn-out photo shots of the King walking up a ramp to a plane, walking down the ramp off the plane or long lines of dignitaries greeting the King. They have long, complicated names such as Sheik (Shake) Yumani ibn Mohammed al-Aziz, , all apparently meaning son of Mohammed, son of Aziz, son of etc., endlessly. The King of the United Kingdom, who constantly paraded back and forth across the screen, was much loved by his people and respected by outsiders. There was no news accompanying his TV presence, only an endless listing of names in Arabic.

All these thoughts raced through my mind as I continued to watch the rehearsal. My fellow country-persons on that stage practising so gaily for their annual social evening, had even somehow adapted themselves to day-by-day living in this timeless legend of scorching sun, endless vistas of sand, and eternity. Only the BBC and the Voice of America, during select hours (very late at night and early a.m. hours), managed to penetrate the shadowy curtain reminding them that there really was a world "out there", that their memories were not an illusion. Mail from the States takes at least ten days, although letters were usually taken to America by travelers or pilots, then mailed with one stamp from there.

After thinking of the drawbacks, but not yet coming up with many pluses, I still didn't have a bona fide answer to the question, "WHY? Again I thought of the one newspaper in English which came in two days late. An unexpected surge of love and patriotism shot through me like an electric shock as I thanked the Lord that I had been born into a land of freedom. At home the news hardly happens before we are watching it replay on our colored TV's. This Arabian adventure could be a traumatic experience, or a therapeutic cleansing, like a back-to-the-land movement--whichever choice moves you. So far no one had explained how the pluses outweighed the minuses, but it wasn't really necessary. What did matter was this supreme adventure for me, acquired through the generosity of Karl and Margaret because they knew I would love it and cherish every moment, which I truly did. Enough of this amateur psychoanalyzing and back to the unique experience.

Now rehearsal was over. I returned to the house about 10:30 and found Karl sprawled out on the living room floor cutting out letters and making other unusual components, i.e., theatre props that I could never have dreamed up. He was spending every available minute creating a "time machine" which involved photography, carpentry, cassette tapes, electronics, the entire back yard and a lot of time and effort. He was creating the heartbeat of this year's Follies-- he was the personification of the backstage person who really made it "go".

"Where's Margaret,?" I asked, but didn't get an immediate answer because Karl was totally engrossed in creating the "time machine".

"I think she went across the street to Janet's to dry her clothes in their dryer. Ours is shot, you know. In fact, I've been passing the word around that we want to buy one if anyone is selling."

"Can't yours be fixed?" I asked thinking that Karl had enough savvy to fix a dryer.

He shook his head, "We can't get parts here, nor anyone to fix appliances. It's simpler to buy another one, although they don't sell them new here, either."

I walked across the dusty street, in through the gate of the cement wall to Janet and Clay's home to see what was happening. A small group was gathered around the bar while tall Clay dispensed "white" or "brown" sidiki to a white-haired Spencer Tracey-like fellow who was introduced to me as Jim S. He said he would soon become Karl's new boss. Karl had recently been promoted and wouldn't be teaching English to the airline employees anymore. Jim was gallant and pleasant. He, in turn, introduced me to a German couple, Ludwig Lou and Dorothea Rattenmeier.

They spoke English with strong German accents. I later found the lady to be very jealous of her husband when he and I got into a spirited conversation about the Moslem religion, which I thought was interesting, but only as a new bit of knowledge. My own religion was completely integrated into my being. Previously, I had only heard of Mecca in a facetious manner, when someone would bow to the "East". But on the bookshelf at the Holt's I found a book which compared the Qu'ran, the holy book of Islam, to the Bible and showed how they paralleled each other.

Lou said that the Prophet Mohammed, who founded the Moslem religion, had been born in Mecca, but when he started evolving his beliefs after studying the Bible as a young man, he was kicked out of Mecca. Today Mecca is Islam's second most revered spot on earth. The great shrine, the Kaaba, is in Mecca and every Moslem is required to visit Mecca at least once in his lifetime. I learned also that Mecca is geographically located about 30 miles from Jiddah which is the gateway for a million Moslems who come from all over the world each year, during the sacred month of Ramadan, to make their once-in-a-lifetime pilgrimage to Mohammed's birthplace.

Lou and I paged through the Qu'ran and found it drew heavily on the Old Testament of the Bible, commenting, judging and elaborating on many of the texts. Many comments were made about Jesus, the great prophet anointed by God, but they disputed his claim to being God or Son of God. It elaborated on the Virgin Mary, with tales of her that we had never seen nor heard.

Lou and I were so engrossed in reading and discussing the Qu'ran versus the Bible that I was taken aback when Dorothea interrupted and remonstrated angrily to him, making a snide remark about me.

Now the front door opened. A couple I hadn't met came in, Chris and Royal, both short, a bit on the stocky side, and plain-looking. Janet introduced me to them, while they explained that they had just come by to see if anyone was going to F.F.'s "night club". So we all trooped out the door like we were following the Pied Piper; except Janet, who was tall and lovely, and Clay. Margaret had gone home at some point in time, so I went with the others over to J.J.'s.

We stayed there awhile and I met Penny and Jerry, a very handsome couple. Penny was thin and dark, and Jerry was medium height, well built and slightly graying. Expletives poured from his mouth like water over a dam, though, and I found it very offensive, although no one else seemed to mind. However, when J.J. said he was tired, Penny and Jerry walked me home. They told me many more interesting anecdotes about Arabians. For instance, if an Arabian man wishes to divorce his wife, he need only say,"I divorce you", three times in the hearing of an official and they are immediately divorced. She then may be exiled from his villa and must find a way to live on her own. He has rights to all children under the age of 14.

"But the Arabs are generous, Jerry said, "If you openly admire anything of theirs, they'll give it to you as a gift".

"They say that's the way King Faisal acquired the palace here in Jiddah. He admired it when visiting the Alireza family. Later, when Sheik Alireza built a new villa, he gave the old one to Prince Faisal. That was before he became King upon the death of his father."

I shook my head in wonderment.

"Why are we standing out here?" Jerry asked. "Let's go to our place and have one more nightcap for the road." By now I had lost all track of time and was game for anything. When Peggy also urged me to come in, we turned around and walked down the sandy lane to their place, only a few houses and across the street from Karl's, .

Their home was very beautiful in contrast to the plain used- furniture type places the others had. They had acquired some marvelous Persian rugs. Everyone owns at least one of the precious rugs because they are accessible and reasonably priced, whereas at home they'd pay a king's ransom for one. Penny was an excellent housekeeper. A look around their home showed me her love and concern for it. Nothing was out of place. Their furniture was lovely--they had bought or imported their beautiful pieces back from their travels.

Penny fixed us a nightcap and again I thought, I never saw such a drinking people in a land where liquor is forbidden. Penny told me about her extraordinary visit with Queen Iffat. "King Faisal has had two real marriages," Penny explained. This Queen is said to be a real love match. I have a friend named Angeline who has somehow formed a friendship with Her Majesty. The Queen invited Angeline and her "friends", an unnamed number, to visit her in her palace. The Queen didn't set a date, but Angeline invited me to be a guest as soon as the time came. We hurried to the suk to one of the material stores. We shopped until we found the exact material to have a dress made which I could wear to visit the Queen. That was Monday. Wouldn't you know," Penny said seriously, "while we were at the suk, the Queen's cousin called and left a message with Jerry at work that we were to come to the new palace outside of town at 5:30 that very day. She said we could wear knee-length skirts or long dresses. Six of us were invited. Of course the dresses wouldn't be ready for several days."

"Whatever did you do, Penny?" I asked.

She shrugged her thin shoulders. "I wore something I already had." Of course seeing this lady who loved perfection, I knew that whatever she wore had been just right. "We took a taxi to the Palace called the Queen's Palace, not the one in the City which was Faisal's Palace because he lives much more frugally than she does."

Jerry brought in another drink and I was so sleepy I could hardly keep my eyes open, but I hung on to Penny's every word because I loved this Cinderella story. My watch read 3:45, but I refused to believe it.

"What happened when you got there?"

Penny shifted and leaned forward sitting comfortably in her beautiful sofa, "We were all seated on couches--the room was lined with them--and we waited for a time for the Queen who finally walked into the room followed by her two cousins who are her personal maids. Iffat is Turkish, by the way and breathtakingly beautiful. As she seated herself, Angeline went to her and pointed each one of us out. We each nodded to her. Then we all sat there, primly, believing she didn't speak English. For thirty minutes, we sat in uncomfortable silence, whispering to each other occasionally. Then, lo and behold, Queen Iffat spoke to us-- would you believe it?--in English. We were astonished and so relieved that we talked with her for an hour and a half. Of course we just answered her questions--I didn't volunteer anything."

Tell me more, Penny," I urged.

Penny appeared to love the impact she was making and she went on, "She had a long dress on, which looked like jersey and she wore a marvelous pendant of jewels around her neck."

"Penny, I think Arabia is truly a land of enchantment. Here you are, just an ordinary American citizen, and you got to meet the Queen of Arabia!"

Penny smiled in a superior sort of way, but I didn't care. I said what I thought and she seemed to love my appreciation. I jumped up then to go, and Jerry and Penny walked me home. It was 5:00 am.

All the lights were blazing in Karl's living room even though the family were all in bed. The doors stood wide open, also, because the weather was a perfect 70 degrees. I smiled groggily, turned the lights off and went to bed. I slept as soundly as if it were my last sleep.

CHAPTER VII

AMERICAN LADY MEETS BEDOUIN WOMEN--RIDES ARABIAN HORSES IN DESERT

What an interesting lady I met tonight! Her adventures have allowed her to know some real Bedouins. I scratched her brain to learn what it was like to talk with those wanderers of the desert, whose lineage dates back to the Patriarchs of the Bible and who still live the same nomadic existence as in ancient times.

Karl had taken me for a ride that evening to the home of the Flannagans who lived on another compound and who had a dryer for sale, as he had learned through the grapevine. A man and a woman both answered our knock on the door, appearing from different directions. They greeted Karl with a friendly "Hello, come on in". I was introduced to Sharon and Vincent. Sharon cordially invited us into a large, sprawling type of house. I couldn't take my eyes off a velveteen painting of a magnificent Arabian horse running wild as if in total surrender to the desert. "Magnificent," I said. Other pictures hanging on the wall were pencil drawings of some typical street scenes in this mysterious land. "Julia Keith, our friend, drew these," Sharon explained, as she saw my great interest.

"Someone loves horses," I commented, because of the number of pictures of marvelous Arabian horses scattered over the living room walls.

"Yes, I do," Sharon surprised me by answering. "Vincent also rides sometimes, but I have a passion for them. They are so beautiful!"

I could picture her sitting astride that beautiful animal in the velveteen picture. Her bright blue eyes which dominated a plain, no make-up face, would probably be looking into the distance as her tall angular figure sat astride the horse dashing out on the sandy desert. She verified my imagination when I asked her where she rode her horse and she answered, "Out in the desert."

"Really?" I asked, never having met anyone who indulged in this interesting hobby.

"Oh, yes," she answered flashing a toothy smile while her thick eyebrows rose in amusement at my uninhibited expression of surprise and awe.

"Do you ever seen any Bedouins out there?" I asked.

"Yes," she answered simply. "I have made friends with some of the Bedouin women."

"How did you do that? I thought that a white person, especially a woman, can't just ride into a Bedouin camp without danger," I said.

"That's true," she nodded. "But sometimes when they are camped in a certain place for quite a few days, I ride up on a nearby hill and just sit there and look at them, day after day, until finally one of the women will venture near me. Of course they wear face masks anytime they're out of their tents."

"Even out in the desert they must cover their faces?" I asked in disbelief.

"Oh, yes," she nodded emphatically. "They are even more strict than the city dwellers. Their masks are just beautiful, though, and are made out of camel leather and hand sewn with beautiful beadwork designs."

Vincent, who was talking to Karl, overheard our conversation and left the room soon to return carrying one of the Bedouin face masks. It was truly beautiful. They were heavy and stiff. It was hard to imagine wearing such a thing over your face in the hot sun of the desert. As I examined this unusual face covering, I had to ask more questions. "What are they like, these ladies of the desert?"

Sharon's blonde hair gleamed in the lamplight as she thought for a minute, then answered, "They are polite and thoughtful. One lady, in a true gesture of friendship wanted to douse my hair with camel urine which they use to keep their hair from drying out in that torturing sun. It's an insult to them to refuse their kindness and it puts a person in a very bad light, but somehow I did manage to avoid accepting that offer--I can't remember how I got out of it, but I did," she laughed softly.

Vincent worked with a geological survey team. He was a dark, stocky, handsome sort of man who showed us aerial views of Bedouin tents and broad views of the endless desert with sudden lifeless black hills or mountains looming unexpectedly on the face of it. He also told tales of flying over the barren land, mapping it and surveying the wild life, taking pictures of herds of goats and camels, which he then developed himself.

Again I had met people who told me of tales I never even dreamed of. I was totally captivated by their adventures. Sharon said she had three very close Arabian lady friends who live in villas in Jiddah. She was the only American person I met who actually had a good social relationship with the native women. Sharon said her friends occasionally telephoned her and invited her to their homes. They would leave a message with Vincent in his office or perhaps at the PCS where Sharon taught, along with Margaret. At this time there was only one phone on Karl's compound. I had also seen one in his office, but that was all.

Sharon told me, "A lady in Arabia, not the desert lady, but a rich woman who lives in a villa and is part of an extended family, spends her day much differently than we do. Her day begins about noon. She often gets up at that time and is served breakfast in her room. Remember, there are many ladies who live in the harem quarters of the house--mothers, mothers-in-law, aunts, children, sisters-in-law and sometimes more than one wife. You see, a man is allowed to have up to four wives."

"And some of them live in the same household?" I asked, aghast at the thought.

"Yes, sometimes," Sharon answered in her straightforward way. "That whole extended family has lunch sometime in the mid-afternoon. Here in the mideast, siesta time is as natural a part of their day as waking up and going to sleep. Usually the men sleep during the hottest hours of the day, while women and children pursue their own enterprises. The men have been up since early morning, engaging in their various businesses. After siesta time, the men take their wives out on some adventure, perhaps horseback riding in the desert or whatever the current fad is for these rich social natives. Most are the King's relatives and are supported by him. About 11 p.m. they go out to have dinner, to a party or to visit friends. They have an incredible variety of parties," she said.

Now Karl said, "Let's go". He and Vincent went out to load the dryer, which Karl had bargained for and bought, into his Toyota station wagon.

"What kind of parties do they have?" I asked, wishing I could stay and listen to these interesting tales forever.

The rich Arabs might be invited for an evening at the Embassy or to a gathering for a visiting official, of which there are endless numbers," she said. "But they are very sweet people." She was now speaking of the city-dwellers and not the Bedouins. Sharon was acquainted with both, and that was really quite unusual from my observations.

As we said goodbye with that last phrase echoing in my ears, Sharon asked me if I'd like to visit the Fish Market on the Red Sea with her on whichever day she could borrow the Geological Survey's driver. I didn't know what the Fish Market was, but I knew it must be interesting. She promised to get in touch soon. Karl and I took off into the dark balmy night with the dryer in the back of the Toyota. It was midnight already.

I hadn't heard a word from home, yet. I had written postcards three days ago; it then took two days to get stamps; Karl then forgot to mail them and, believe me, there were no mailboxes on the street corners in Arabia. Hopefully tomorrow would be the "big day" and they would get mailed. When they'd arrive in Minnesota was anybody's guess.

I sent an airgram with a lady who left for the States tonight, besides the telegram Karl sent the other day. I panic inwardly over the impossibility of getting in touch with my family or, they with me, in case of an emergency . My son was still young and at home with his father, and my daughter, Anne was married to Harold, a wonderful elementary schoolteacher. They had two daughters. I couldn't dwell on that or I'd ruin my trip. My world back home seemed like a faraway dream that didn't even belong to me right then. Strange, but true.

Margaret had flown to Beirut, Lebanon, on Tuesday for a doctor's appointment. She hadn't been feeling well, was tired, losing weight and generally rundown. She only weighed about 98 pounds and she might fade away if she lost anymore. The casualness of her journey amazed me. She packed a little overnight bag, left the house about 1:30 p.m, and walked to the airport two blocks away to take a 2:30 plane. It had to fly over two countries to get to that figurative Mecca of the mideast called Beirut. I heard there was no place in the world like Lebanon. It not only has perfect climate with lush oversized fruits and the legendary Cedars of Lebanon, but you could get anything you wanted there. It's almost too easy to buy prescription drugs which were available without a prescription, for a little money. One can go there, live for a weekend in lavish surroundings, with every forbidden or desired luxury as close as the telephone in your beautiful hotel room. But, Margaret walked off just as casually as if she were running across the street during Leila's nap, while Julie and Terry were in school and Karl was at work. I was baby-sitting and appreciated being able to help out.

Karl and the two older girls were at the movie, Leila was sleeping and it was therapeutic for me to sit there quietly, and gather my thoughts together. I felt almost breathless, having not had many moments to sum up the new experiences that had been hitting me like sleeting rain.

Chris Speake invited us for supper earlier that evening. Her husband Bill and son, Sandy were still in the States visiting his folks, so just Chris and her youngest son, Careme, age six, were home. Chris outdid herself with a steak filet and a special rice hot dish. It was delicious. I loved looking around their home which was filled with a myriad of fascinating mementos from different parts of the world. They had collected everything from beautiful hand tooled trunks and Persian rugs, to paintings, wall hangings, etc. There was no one here who was not a "citizen of the world". Fascinating people.

I was longing for some news from the outside world, but I couldn't get anything from the radio at that early hour. We were three hours ahead of Europe and nine ahead of America. I'd been in Jiddah more than a week already, but still had not heard a word from home. I hadn't seen a paper for three days. When it did come, it would be at least two days old. In order to keep my serenity, I had to accept the spirit of "malesh". It was a reflection of the timelessness of the desert and this civilization, which still retained its age old culture in spite of the new technology they had to have, to continue to hold their lead in this third world. I could imagine that communication was almost nonexistent before the advent of the jets. It even seemed so now. The concept behind "malesh" is like faith. One can accept it intellectually, but to really feel it, believe it and live it at a gut level is hard-- and doesn't descend on you overnight.

There was an Arabian, no, Egyptian, movie on TV right then. At least it was something different, but I wished it were in English.

CHAPTER VIII

FISH MARKET ADVENTURE-WOMEN NOT WELCOME. YEMENIE SUK FRIGHTENING

The fish market was unexpectedly frightening, with some tense and fearful moments. No wonder women never go to the fish market by the Red Sea. Only an adventuresome person like Sharon Flannagan would attempt it.

We left early this morning when Sharon's African-born driver, a dear old black man named Joseph, drove Sharon, Karen Fillenbaum, a young married American who teaches French in the PCS school, and me, to the site of the forbidden (to women) fish market. What a scene! A large crowd gathered under a square canvas that topped an open-air booth. Every part of this open tent had some kind of fish hanging from it. The men, a motley group made up of many nationalities, were wearing their native costumes. The color of their skin ranged from swarthy to black. The sun shone in dazzling splendor, but the cacophony made by the crowd sounded like an ominous buzz. As our driver drove near this scene, the men turned around and literally glared at us with great hostility. Many police guards stood outside the crowd. We did get out of the car in spite of the evident animosity. The few pictures I was able to take were very quick and discreet. I wouldn't have gotten any, if I hadn't had my small instamatic camera that I could draw swiftly out of my purse to snap a scene in a second. In spite of the malodorous smell, I strained my eyes to find the different kinds of sea inhabitants that Sharon was pointing out to me, such as squid, groupers, barracuda, shark, a hamure, resembling a sea bass, and sawfish. She added they also sold turtle and shrimp. I found it hard to concentrate on her words because of the many hostile eyes glaring at us.

"You are really brave, Sharon, " I whispered, and Karen, tall, thin, dark hair pulled straight back and hanging long down her back, agreed with a nod of her head. We then

A VARIETY OF FISH HANGING IN
THE OPEN AIR FISH MARKET

ANGRY ARAB GLARING AT US IN THE FISH MARKET-
-WOMEN NOT ALLOWED

JALOUSIES OR SHUTTERED BALCONIES
FOR WOMEN OF A HAREM

ENTRANCE TO PCS WHERE THE WESTERN CHILDREN
ATTEND SCHOOL. MARGARET TEACHES HERE

walked down to the sea where the unimaginably terrible fishy smell was less potent.

Men, in their long thobes were pounding nails into wood forming it into seaworthy boats. They didn't look up from their work. Half- hearted hammering echoed along the shore where others were building either fishing boats or pearling ships. I wondered how they ever got them finished at the slow pace they worked. Walking along, I had a hard time not showing surprise at the squalid shacks that resembled huge overturned shipping crates, squares cut in them for window openings.

"I leaned over and whispered a question in Sharon's ear, "Do people really live in those?"

In a whisper she answered, "Yes, and I'm sure we are being closely watched from them. Be very careful not to take any pictures now." It was really scarry. Debris and garbage littered the sandy shore. I understood why the King wouldn't want those scenes photographed and taken out of the country.

We hurried back toward the fish market again where Joseph idled the car waiting for us. It was a tense walk and I gratefully climbed into the car. Again the stench of fish hit me like a ton of bricks. I digress: my sense of smell is acute; I remembered that one of my secret fears when contemplating this trip was that some odors might be so bad here in Arabia that I might actually get sick. A foolish notion perhaps, but to me smell is my most sensitive sense. Until now I hadn't noticed an odious smell that really offended my nose.

We closed our car door and Joseph hurried past the booth. I quickly snapped a picture of the crowd and the fish, but sharp eyes spotted my small camera and, just as we sped away, many men came rushing after our car, shaking their fists and shouting angryly at us. I made sure the car doors were secure while Sharon seemed cool and collected, as did Joseph, but Karen looked scared and remained silent.

Sharon, who had experienced much of this before, shrugged her rugged shoulders and told us, "Vince and I were here by the Red Sea one day and we snapped photos of those shacks near the shore. Before we knew it, the camera was ripped out of Vince's hand and some men tore the film out of it."

"Did you get your camera back?" Karen asked, unknowingly confirming my inexperienced observations that Sharon Flannagan took a lot of risks that other westerners dared not try.

"We did, but we had to go to the police station. It was fortunate that we got it back and were not further restricted. We lost our film, though. I heard about one American who shot some film of a forbidden scene. He was followed home by the police, who seemed to emerge from nowhere. They practically broke into his house, rifled all his files and destroyed many of them.

Surely this day couldn't hold more excitement than this, I thought, but Sharon had planned a further expedition that was just as unexpected and frightening. She asked Joseph to drive into the "old Yemenie suk". Joseph looked her right in the eye as if to ascertain if she were serious. When that dear old black man saw that she meant it, (Sharon did not fool around), he guided the car through the sandy paths hardly wide enough for a car, not even a real road. Truly the tales of Aladdin must have originated here. Our car wound down the dusty trail, past dirty Arab men, veiled women, black ladies carrying urns on their heads and an African lady sitting in the hot sun selling seed beads. We had Joseph stop the car and we bought several chains of them. We were in such alien territory that a crowd gathered to watch us and children followed us, smiling shyly as though we had arrived from another planet.

We walked now, while Joseph dutifully followed in the car. We saw a camel, my first glimpse of the one-humped dromedary. Disappointment flooded my being. The poor old flea-bitten skinny drudge labored all day under the sweltering sun, not knowing that he was attached to a cylinder and walking in a circle. "He doesn't know that he walks in circles all day making the energy needed to mash chickpeas into mash or 'homos' (homus)", explained

Sharon. "Everyone dunks his unleavened bread chunks into homos, a general term covering different kinds of mash. Some of it is made from soybeans. We use butter, they use homos."

The smell of a camel is indescribably bad. I managed to snap a picture of his skinny old rump while the master hollered at us that the Government forbids all pictures.

We continued on then, down the dried, crusty, dusty streets, passing open stalls in which merchants sold spices which most of us in America only see in labeled jars or cans. Many whole spices like cardamon, cinnamon, aloes, mhyrr, frankincense, gum arabic, saffron, big chunks of alabaster as well as others, were sold by dark-eyed men in their checkered headscarves. We were in a world so ancient and totally unfamiliar, that later I would shake my head and ask myself if it had been a dream or a reincarnation of some ancient time. Since Sharon had an appointment at noon, I hardly had time to digest this ancient suk. I snapped a picture of three beautiful, shy little girls, who had followed us all the way down the dusty trail of a street; then we climbed back into the car. Slowly Joseph wound his way through the treacherous street out of that forgotten moment in time that had never progressed from the unrecorded days of Caliphs, Emirs and Vizers.

While I still contemplated that strange old Yemenie suk, Karen offered to go to the material suk with me to buy material for a long dress i.e., galibea (gal-i-bee-a). It would be an acceptable dress for any occasion while I was here, plus an interesting memento for me to take home. Consequently, Karen and I were soon back in the regular suk, going from store to store feeling textures and pricing materials. I had never seen so many varieties of beautiful fabrics. We finally settled on a certain material for myself and also some for my married daughter, Anne Marie, back home. The fat, smiley tailor measured Karen for Anne Marie's dress as she was a size 10, the same size as my red - headed daughter. Her material was six riyals a meter and we found that she needed 3-1/2 meters. My material was 5 riyals a meter. The tailor charged 20 riyals apiece to sew them, about $6.50 each. Good price! It wasn't bad for two long dresses of lovely material. "Come back in four days," he told us, smiling as he bowed from his portly waist.

"Do you want to go to lunch?" Karen asked as we walked out in the sandy walkway.

"Oh yes, but where?" I asked, never having seen a restaurant except those coffee houses where the men sat and smoked their hubbly-bubblies and drank coffee. "I'm starved."

"I'll show you." Karen led the way to a building near the suk and we entered a different kind of eating place, unlike any that I had ever seen. First we walked through a narrow hallway made bright by stained glass windows, with a waterfall cascading over rocks outside. Walking up a wide marble stairway curving elegantly at the top, we entered a room which featured more opaque windows through which sunlight filtered through the waterfall! Our feet touched marble flagstone floors as we were escorted ceremoniously by a bowing turbanned waiter, to one of the little round tables, each in a separate little cove. It was strange, but lovely.

I waited for Karen to clue me in on what to order. There was an Arabian menu, but Karen knew what to do and after asking me if I liked chicken she ordered each of us a chicken dinner. Karen was really kind of cute, even with her too-thin long face and tightly pulled back dark hair, which she wore in two pony tails today. She seemed very young, but must have been in her late twenties. Karen had evinced an unusual interest in the fact that I was a writer, and had loved my long narrative poem, *My Proctor*, portraying the small town where I grew up and lived now. I appreciated her interest, as does any writer whose works are read and absorbed.

Soon the waiter came back with round unleavened loaves of Arabian bread which we pulled apart and dunked in a homos mixture of gisch. I think the bread is tasteless, but Karen assured me that I would actually hunger for it when I got used to it. Maybe, I thought! While we waited for our broiled chicken, (chicken seems to be the universal food of the world), a gargantuan man came puffing up the stairs. Immediately he recognized Karen and ceremoniously sat down with us. She introduced me to Sulaimen, owner of the cafe. He was effusive and charming, chatting with us in English while being affectionate toward Karen. As he rose to leave us, he planted a noisy wet kiss on each of our cheeks and invited us to come for lunch as his guests the next time.

Just then a startling event took place in the guise of a tall masterly figure. He came whirling into view up the marble stairs causing me to catch my breath. A Sheik (shake), with his black cape swirling about him and his black headbands on his white ghutra, looked very impressive as he quickly swept the room with his fierce dark eyes. Then he motioned his lady up the stairs. She appeared, veiled from top to toe and they sat in the booth next to ours. His presence in that room was almost overwhelming. I watched in fascination as the lady took off her veil and looked me right in the eyes. I turned away after smiling at her, but both Karen and I watched them furtively. The lady was quite pretty, with dark eyes, black hair and olive skin, but the Sheik's presence seemed to shout of his virility, lending an air of excitement to that quiet upstairs cafe. I wished I could meet him.

The broiled chicken was good, but we didn't eat the accompanying dinner salad because I had been cautioned not to eat any lettuce outside the home, for dysentery would surely follow. After we ate, we went downstairs where Karen paid the owner as he sat at the cash register near the door. She tendered a 20 riyal bill. After giving her back the change, he came around and again kissed us on our cheeks, and reiterated his invitation for dinner the next day. Only after we were outside did Karen count her money and found that he had given it all back to her in change. We had eaten for free. "How nice of him", we said at the same time.

We were surprised to feel a wind had come up. The sun was hiding behind a dark ominous cloud and little bits of sand were swirling about. As Karen asked me what I'd like to see next, a man in a tower began to sing a toneless chant. Karen said he was a muezzin and was calling all to come to prayer. We were standing very close to the door of a mosque and could see right into it. Many men were closing down their shops and literally running to the house of prayer. They lined up in rows, chanted together, knelt down, touched their heads to the floor and bowed toward Mecca. Now I knew what our old half-humorous gesture of bowing to the east meant--it was bowing toward Mecca, the center of Moslem belief, and old as the sands of the desert. Karen cautioned me that I must keep walking, but I stayed a moment to watch as the white-robed men knelt down bowing and praying to Allah.

"Come on, the wind will blow us away", she said, grabbing my hand, because the swirling sand was blinding me now as I ran along beside her. Almost all the stalls were closed because it was prayer time and we gasped as we hurried up the narrow shadowy paths that lead from street to street. I was completely disoriented in this place. There was no way to find one's direction and it seemed like an enclosed world of its own. Then we saw a booth that was open so we went in. I found some souvenirs that fit my pocketbook and needs. I found a camel whip to bring home to my son, Johnny, costing 15 riyals. The handle was hand carved with a rich mosaic pattern tooled into the braided leather. The top unscrewed, yielding a sharp ice-pick pointed end that could take your eye out in a second--a nice little toy. I also bought 2 hand carved cigarette boxes made in Carache for 12 riyals. I bargained with the proprietor for an abia (black silk floor-lenth cape) and a black veil, the costume of the Arabian lady on the street. He asked 50 riyals for that , but I haggled with him and bought it for 22 riyals.

The little basket boys had continued to follow us ever since we got to the suk. We had been reiterating, "la shukron," meaning, "No, thank you," to them. There were many boys from 8-16 who literally pestered us to hire them until finally we did hire one boy for awhile. He was a darling little brown-eyed, curly-haired 14 year old who showed us where to go and advised us about prices and what we should pay for our purchases. He also acted as our bargaining agent when the merchant didn't speak English. Faisal put our packages in his basket which he perched on his head. Finally we paid him two riyals just to leave us alone to wander where we would. The very small children also followed us, touching us on the arm with their little brown hands held out for money.

By now, the late afternoon sky had become very clouded and unusually dark. The wind whipped sand into our eyes until I couldn't open mine to see where I was going. Karen and I searched desperately for a taxi. Usually untold numbers of them plied the streets, but now there were none in sight. I now knew that a good old fashioned Minnesota snow blizzard was preferable to a sand blizzard, because snow doesn't sting you so, nor hurt your eyes as much as one grain of sand does. We were both exhausted, too. It had been a long, busy day. In fact, it seemed like a week since we had left the compound early this morning to experience the fish market.

We both shouted at once as we hailed the one taxi that drove into view. It was a "souped up" vehicle, complete with all kinds of gadgets plus an extra horn to add to the din of the horn-blowing drivers on the busy Abdul Aziz Boulevard. The driver charged 2 riyals and we shouted, "Shukron," i.e., "Thank you" as we ran into the Wombacher home with a great sigh of relief.

Karl was home babysitting Leila who had just awakened from her afternoon nap. Before I had time to catch my breath, Karen walked out the door on her way to her home close by. Her young school teacher husband apparently awaited her.

Karl said, "Guess what? Caroline Rathbone returned from the States a couple of days ago. I'm anxious for you to meet her. She's probably out of the jet lag syndrome by now. Do you want to drive over now?"

I was still sand-blown from the storm. It seemed to me I had experienced enough for one day, but still I thought I'd better go when the opportunity presented itself, so the three of us climbed into Karl's little car and on to another interesting adventure.

We drove across the city through the constant, busy, noisy traffic and the never-ceasing honking and unlawful, aggressive drivers. As we approached the villa, a bit of daylight still remained and now I could see the wide marble stairways. The place was as large as a magnificent mansion, surrounded by a six foot high cement wall.

We walked around the villa to the back yard where we found Rodion working on his boat. He looked up from pounding nails to greet us and Karl joked about the fact that he had been working on it for three years. Rodion's shorts had a large tear from the thigh up, but Rodion didn't appear to care. I snapped a photo of Rodion, Karl and Leila beside his craft which would soon, hopefully, be seaworthy. He put his tools aside and led us upstairs to meet Caroline. She wasn't the person I had pictured her to be. (I was so exhausted at this time that the story of meeting Caroline had to be written later. In retrospect at I think no day could have been more packed with new experiences).

CHAPTER IX

PSYCHOLOGICAL GAME REVEALS UNIVERSAL TRUTHS ABOUT OURSELVES

Back to my meeting with Caroline Rathbone. Rodion led us down the long art lined hallway into the living room at the far end. A fragile gray-haired lady came forward to meet us. Her hair was pulled straight back from her face with a pink ribbon tied around her head while the remainder fell abundantly over her shoulders, thin and silky. As she hugged Karl, I noticed her unusually bright eyes and transparent white skin. Karl introduced us over the blaring of a record player. She greeted me warmly while shouting above the noise, that her favorite song was playing, not offering to turn it down. Immediately she asked Karl if he would see if he could find what was causing a particular noise problem in it. Karl, being good natured and usually happy to please, began to "dig" into it. Meanwhile, Rodion, who had unobtrusively disappeared during the greetings came back with some glasses of the "Rodion specials". He was very congenial and still had the brief torn shorts on.

The classical music was raucously loud and conversation was impossible, which struck me as strange. Caroline, a wisp of a woman, turned her attention to Leila who was crying. Caroline handed her the matches she was reaching for, proclaiming, "There's no such thing as 'no' in this house." She lit her cigarette dramatically.

In a complete change of mood, she turned to me and said, "Wait until I show you the dress I bought just to go with my necklace". I had noticed her necklace earlier but because of the music hadn't mentioned how gorgeous I thought it was, even on the short multicolored duster of woven material. It was made of silver, adorned with lovely colored gems, flaring out into three separated finger-like pieces, truly a treasure. "This is my present from Rodion for our thirty-third wedding anniversary. You see," she said half wistfully and half jokingly, "It takes that long to get anything this beautiful". It puzzled me. Then she whirled out of the room, soon to return carrying a beautiful brown suede dress with which to wear her lovely jewelry. "Stunning!" she said dramatically and I agreed. Again she disappeared down the long hallway calling over her shoulder for me to come to her bedroom where the disorganization of her unpacking and other things that had long been stacked made it almost impossible to get into the room. But she wanted to show me some dresses she had bought in New York at a shop where famous people such as Liza Minnelli and others brought their discarded clothes. She quickly paraded a tweed suit before me. Then she brought out a skirt she had "picked up" in India, insisting that I try it on to really know how comfortable it was. Again we returned to the spacious living room where Karl had succeeded in fixing her record player and had shut it off. Thank God! We all sat down wherever we could, by moving some things off a chair.

Caroline told us about the fantastic man she met on the plane. Most of it was what she said to him, not much of his replies. When we left, I hardly knew what to think of this dramatic lady, except it had been an interesting encounter. I said to Karl as we rode through the City in his car, "She is different than I expected". Karl expressed surprise, but I didn't elaborate although I did qualify that I liked her.

Tonight, I was baby sitting the girls while Karl and Margaret went to the movie on the compound, Two People , with Peter Fonda. Margaret had returned from Beirut today as unobtrusively as she had left two days ago. Ten minutes after they left, Rodion and Caroline came walking in the front door. Caroline wore a lovely long thobe, that dress usually worn by Arab men, but adapted by western ladies to their own wardrobes. She wore her lovely necklace like a badge of honor.

"I'll run to the movie compound and get Karl and Margaret. They'd rather see you than see the movie," I said. I knew their visit was rare, but both protested the idea, sat themselves down on the couch and talked with me. We discussed a variety of subjects, mostly impersonal, such as the current movie rage in America which was The Exorcist.

Rodion was curious about its theme. I explained it a bit, about the demon possession, admitting I had read the book but ended up burning it. "I have never done such a thing in my life," I told them, "But I didn't want to be responsible for anyone picking up that tale of the devil in my house." This immediately brought on questions of why I felt like this. I told them that I believed people could be possessed, also paraphrasing one line of the book which stated that unless you have knowledge of "possession" it can't happen. I think the less one knows about witchcraft and demons, the better off they are," I said. "Do you know how gleefully the papers print the number of people who get sick, vomit or faint while watching this movie and yet hundreds rush to the movie to see if it will happen to them?" I stopped abruptly.

Just then Julie and Terry trouped in, fresh and rosy from their nightly bath. The Rathbones greeted them with much affection. Then they were off to bed.

As Caroline excused herself to go to the washroom, I walked over by the bookshelf. The paperback, *The Meaning of Success*, literally leaped out at me--one of my favorite books. I picked out the Michael Quoist book asking Rodion if he ever heard of it or read it. That book had taught me a lot about what success was all about.

"Do you have a religious background, Rodion?" I asked, feeling able to talk to him about this.

"I was brought up in the Church of England," he answered, "But the restrictions totally turned me off and I didn't really maintain any religious belief. Later in my life, I studied all the great religions, but didn't find any satisfactory answers. When I came to the mideast, I found a philosophy I could live by." Caroline returned now and I didn't pursue that statement, although I was curious about it.

Rodion stood up ready to leave then, but Caroline didn't want to go. "Maybe Karl will give me a ride home later," she said.

"I"m sure he will," I said. So Rodion apologized, smiled shyly and left.

Only five minutes later, Karl and Margaret returned from the movie and brought four people with them. I hadn't met them before, they were teachers associated with P.C.S. Margaret introduced Caroline and me to the two couples. They sat down after the amenities when an extremely tall, handsome young man ducked into the doorway. He was their next door neighbor, Clel, a mechanic for Saudi Airlines, who, like Karl and the others was actually employed by TWA. He, like the others, was leased to the Saudis. "Clel's wife, Becky, is the tall beautiful young woman who is doing the choreography for the Follies," Karl explained. They all liked Karl a lot. He was kind, intelligent, straightforward and didn't have an egotistical bone in his body. Clel folded his 6'7" form down beside me in one of the last chairs Karl could find in the house, when in walked Jan, who wandered in and out many times a day. He found himself a spot on the floor. Caroline, usually adverse to crowds these days, seemed to have a wonderful time talking to everyone. You never knew when there would be company around here. It was fun. I talked to Clel, or rather he talked to me, telling me about his life and how he met his wife, Becky, back in California, and how they longed to go back there and buy themselves a little dream house.

After the others left and only Caroline, Clel and I were left, Karl and Margaret thought of a game they wanted us to play. It proved to be an interesting psychological game, but they didn't warn us of that. They asked us questions about the kind of house we'd choose to live in, where it would be located, what kind of driveway would come up to the house., what kind of trees we'd like and where they'd be located in relationship to our chosen house. Each of us had very different ideas.

Not one of the three of us realized until later that we were revealing our very secret psychological selves. Caroline described her house as a wonderful log house on a rugged ocean coastline where she could hear the roaring of the surf. It would be surrounded by high private shade trees and access would be difficult. There was much more, but I didn't write it all down and have forgotten all she said, except her choices revealed that she was a very private person and didn't want anyone close to her and perhaps the

70

roaring of the surf was a sign of great unrest in her soul.

Clel touched my heart with his idea of a dream house. This giant-sized, handsome young man was really sweet. His dream house was the house he and Becky longed to buy situated in California. It was a bungalow with a winding sidewalk to the small front porch with cute little windows through which one could look out at the world. It sounded like the American dream for the common man, just to be happy and part of the universe, close to your family. I found myself genuinely liking this sincere young giant who appeared to be in his late 30's.

I opted for a large house, a manor with many rooms, some not even known yet. A long winding driveway, lined by high palm trees, would bring you up to my house, the back of which was hidden in close knit shade trees that touched each other and also closed in on my palatial estate. Karl interpreted my fancies that I still felt I had many things to explore in life in my house of many rooms, that I wanted people to think I was aloof or independent because of the winding road lined with tall trees leading up to my house, but the shade tree in back might mean that I loved my friends and needed them close to me.

There was much more interpretation for all of us, but I summarize only a part of it because of the three people involved, pointing out the great differences in our makeup, all of us converging in this far corner of the earth--in Jiddah, Saudi Arabia.

Later, as Margaret and Karl visited with Caroline, Clel and I became better acquainted. Surprisingly we had much to discuss. We were both very interested in each other's backgrounds and time and age fell away to disclose two souls who met in a euphoria of timelessness. When tall Clel left, he said that he felt I was a person who cared about others. "I knew from the moment I entered this room," he said and for the first time in years my innermost being felt a thrill and a longing for his next words. "You had an unusual look in your eyes--a caring look," he said and looked down at me with serious eyes. At that very moment he took his place in my heart as one of my life's unforgettable people. I was to see Clel again.

We drove through this exciting city at midnight as we took Caroline home. I never expected to see a city so lively. Stores were open. Barbers were cutting hair in their little open-air shops, and men were socializing while sipping coffee in the outdoor cafes. Even fruit stands were open for business. I found this quite opposite from the world I had come from. Of course it had never occurred to me that the Arabs rested during the zenith of the hot day, only to come alive in the coolness of the evening. Common sense would tell us this, but it revealed to me how little I had ever known of this far side of the world. Soon we let Caroline off and watched her get safely inside her door, although no one worries about prowlers or rapists here. There is very little crime. Karl said if a person were caught stealing he would likely have his hand cut off in a public display to prove that crime is not worth the cost. "If you see a man with only one hand, you'll know he's a thief," Karl said with a grin. "There's no need for punishment very often," he added.

As we drove through dark narrow little streets lined by walled-in houses and villas, we occasionally spotted a mysterious white figure slipping into one of the gates. Darkness and mystery caused me to shiver with a mixture of fear and delight.

The days seemed to pass much too fast. I tried to savor every wonderful minute of it. The next day Karl and Jan were taking me on a scuba diving expedition to the Red Sea. Exciting expectations!

KARL AND WIFE MARGARET CHAT
WITH CAROLYN RATHBONE

MONEY CHANGER IN MARKET PLACE (SUK)

CORAL REEF IN THE RED SEA PHOTOGRAPHED BY KARL

CHRIS SPEAKE WITH COMPANION SCUBA
DIVERS ABOUT TO DIVE INTO THE RED SEA

CHAPTER X

NO "PARTING OF THE RED SEA" BUT SCUBA DIVING EXCITING, TOO

The scuba diving trip to the Red Sea was exciting and even dangerous, I thought. Two cars left the compound at 11 a.m. and drove around the city enroute to the Sea. There are few maps in Jiddah, so it's difficult to get one's bearings. Karl and I rode in his car while Jan Copeland, Chris Speake and a young German fellow named Hans rode in Jan's. We were heading for the Raytheon compound. Karl explained that the Arabs guarding the gate to the compound might be difficult to pass and the place where they would dive was inside this gate. We drove through a long stretch of desert as he was explaining this. This was the first time I had really seen the arid sandy desert and I watched with great interest as we drove.

Then we were at the guard station. A visitor has to prove he is going to visit one of the employee's homes in order to pass through the security station, which resembles the toll gate on an interstate highway, by having the guards call and verify his anticipated arrival. Strangely enough, the Raytheon employees seemed to have phones, while only one TWA employee had a phone at this time. Jan gave the name of a certain doctor he was acquainted with, but no one answered the phone. Jan thought of one more person he knew on the compound, but again no response. The Saudi guards looked very hostile, both hands on their guns, eyeing us ominously. I was scared, hardly daring to move. We waited 20 minutes while the combined brains of all the scuba divers tried to think of the name of someone they knew. Finally they came up with a name of a resident of the compound and the person was home. This person verified knowing Jan and at last the magic gate opened. We passed through with a united sigh of relief. It seems that fooling around with Saudis is always a bit risky--like VERY! Our two cars followed a long narrow road; we passed the airstrip and employee homes along the way, and drove out onto a long peninsula about a mile until we came to a huge decaying cement pier, and there was the beautiful Red Sea. I saw its color which was a joyous azure blue in the shallows, but off the cement pier which was half falling into the Sea, it was a deep pure blue. The waves lapped against the pier; a dancing wind blew, making the day warm and exciting; the sun was at its zenith. It was great, even though there was a smell of fish or garbage here.

Chris was the only female diver and I thought she was very brave, especially after I found out what diving entailed. They all proceeded in a businesslike manner to strap oxygen tanks on their backs, slip flippers on their feet, and don their face masks. One by one they jumped off the pier with a splash. I expected them to bob around on the surface, but they immediately disappeared below the water. In seconds the water covered their tracks and there was no sign of them. It was rather frightening because I, in no way, had been prepared for their complete disappearance, nor could I even guess how long they'd be gone. Furtively, I watched the road, too, noting that there was no place to hide if some soldiers did come down that mile-long, narrow treeless road. A car did appear and I prayed as it came closer. What would I say if someone confronted me as to why I was here? I couldn't pretend I was driving one of those cars because women are forbidden to drive in Arabia. My fears were dispelled when it turned out to be an American male. We conversed a bit. He said he was just out for a ride and lived on the Raytheon compound. He left shortly. To pass some time, I found some ugly coral and shells washed up by the side of the pier and collected some just because they were from the Red Sea. I sat down and tried to remember some of the biblical stories about it. I meditated on the cement pier which was slashed by a deep incision caving inward. I thought of it as a symbol of its unworthiness to stand in the legendary Red Sea. I watched the playful waves as they turned from transparent aquamarine to a deep blue as the water deepened. My mind played a little game of trying to picture what had happened to the thousands of Egyptian soldiers who had followed Moses, the leader of the Israelites, on their journey to the promised land, when the Sea rolled back and they were all drowned. The innocently playful splashing of the waves was really deceiving because it was truly the tomb of thousands of people. Was I really here gazing into these very biblical waters? Would Karl and the others never come back? Time seemed endless and there was nothing to do, nor even a good place to sit because the pier was so lopsided.

Speaking of a tomb, I feared to ask myself what had happened to the scuba divers. They had been gone 45 minutes now and there was no sign they would ever return. I stuffed my fears, not daring to go a step further and ask the inevitable question, "What would I do if they never emerged?" I wished Karl had prepared me for this. I didn't know what to expect. How long would they be gone?

The decaying pier was surrounded by rubble and stones. Across the way I could see the outline of Jiddah. All was still except for the sound of the gentle waves. Time hung heavy now and I picked up a few more fossilized shells. I thought of all the great ocean and sea-going vessels that daily brought imports into Jiddah from India, Africa, Europe, America, and from all the far-flung world over these many years. For centuries Arabia had exported and imported spices from the Far East. This same gentle sea that I gazed upon this dazzlingly beautiful sunny day in February had seen thousands of years of history. It had even been here during the time of Adam and Eve. Legend says and the Koran proclaims that Eve supposedly walked through the Red Sea after Adam died at Mt. Ararat and fell onto the shore of the place later called Jiddah, i.e., "Grandmother". Historically this very sea had been sailed on by Abraham, David, all the Biblical patriarchs and even, perhaps, Jesus.

I pondered many things in that solitary hour or more while I waited, lonely and fearful, on that forbidden pier on the edge of the Red Sea, not fully understanding why it was forbidden for them to scuba dive here. Home was also on my mind. If it was noon here, it would be about 3 a.m. in

Minnesota. This scene seemed unbelievable as I gazed at the cloudless blue sky and felt the warm wind blow across my face. I thought of my married daughter, Anne, who lived about 40 miles from us. She would soon wake up Harold, her school teacher husband to send him off to school and bundle up little dark haired Lori to go to kindergarten. Lori was a miniature little Anne except for her fluff of dark hair, whereas Anne's hair was coppery colored. That little blonde minx of a Julie, 3 years old who would be home with Anne all day. I missed them a lot. I knew it was impossible for any of them to visualize me sitting on a broken down cement pier, my legs dangling in the warm water, gazing nostalgically out over the sea and wondering where the scuba divers were.

Then, down the narrow ribbon of road, a cloud of dust came steadily toward me. Closer and closer it came as my heart beat rapidly. Not even a bush around--I must suffer the consequences of whoever came. A lone motorcyclist emerged from behind the cloud. He stopped the cycle, swung himself off, walked to the opposite side of the pier from where I sat and looked into the water without even glancing my way. I breathed easier when I saw he wasn't a soldier. Perhaps he may have been an American, but I couldn't see his face. Shortly after, he climbed on his motorcycle and rode away in another cloud of dust. I didn't know what to think. "<u>Why don't they come back</u>?" I asked aloud to the empty sea and sky.

This Red Sea also touches on Israel, I continued to ponder. I knew I must pray to the Holy Spirit about going to Jerusalem because I couldn't conceive of being on this side of the world and not going to the cradle of Christendom and yet , how could I do that? What a dilemma!

I thought back six months ago when I had asked myself what I would truly like to do in my lifetime if I had a choice. I was praying at that time for guidance and the answer that came to me was that I wished to walk in the Holy Land once in my life. At the time I thought it was impossible. I was a middle-class housewife working to supplement the family income, with a young son at home and an unadventurous husband, but I was convinced the Holy Spirit could bring about anything if it was right for a person. I offered this desire to the triune God and almost forgot about it.

It came back to me three months later, when Karl's unexpected invitation arrived in the mail. And now here I was in Saudi Arabia, but ironically, for all intents and purposes, a trip to Israel was as seemingly out of the question as it had been back home. The only place on this whole earth that Karl and Margaret and their co-workers couldn't go was to Jerusalem. If they ever entered that Jewish land, they could never, ever reenter any Arab nation. Karl couldn't even utter the name of Jerusalem in his conversation for fear of reprisal.

Now, today, while gazing out over the historic and utterly beautiful Red Sea, I reflected on how I had barely gathered together $300 for my month overseas, against my husband's wishes, how costly Paris had been, even on the budget rate, while I waited for my plane to Jiddah, and how very low my funds were running. How then would I ever get to Jerusalem? Time was running out, too. I had no answer. On a human level there was no solution. But, as I had learned so many times, when you can't solve the problem, you put it in the hands of the Lord. Again I prayed, believing if there was a way, it would come about or the path which I should take would be shown to me.

My reverie was interrupted when, with a splash, Karl surged up to the side of the pier. I was overjoyed to see him and I ran over to help him up on the pier. "I had no idea you'd be gone this long," I said as I checked my watch and saw it had been an hour and 30 minutes.

"I ran out of oxygen," he said breathlessly. "I thought you knew that scuba diving was deep-sea diving. Anyway, I just saw my first school of barracuda," he said excitedly, as he continued to gasp for breath.

"Really? Aren't they dangerous?"

"Man-eaters," he said, semi-seriously. "I also saw my first shark, and an angel fish which clings to the coral and is pretty deadly also."

"Karl, it's dangerous down there. You're really brave!" I

couldn't imagine myself walking under water into that kind of danger. I get claustrophobic in closed places and the fear of being underwater and not being able to get away made me shiver, in spite of the bright sun and warm breeze.

"About ten feet from the pier, there's a coral reef that drops off to about 70 feet," Karl pointed to the deeper blue water a short distance out.

I shook my head in awe. "I can't imagine myself doing that," I said, as a little cloud covered the sun and the wind blew a bit ominously. Then the others started bobbing up from the deep. One by one they returned, each with his/her own story of adventure. Chris had seen a school of sharks from within ten feet. Hans had lost his sense of direction. Then Jan, the diving teacher, showed up. They all pulled themselves up on the deformed pier and took off their gear. I cast my eyes over the sea again. I thought that I was in love with that fantastic, legendary body of water whose gently lapping waves deceptively covered the treachery and debauchery of mankind that it had witnessed in its long span upon this mortal earth. It was tranquil now.

On the way back to the compound, we passed the modern Parents Cooperative School (PCS) which Karl's girls attended and where Margaret had taught English and Business Training before Leila was born. Karl noted that someone was in the school, in spite of its being Thursday, the weekend, as a car was parked in the courtyard. We stopped and went up the wide stairs and into Principal John Kopp's office. He was at his desk, working. Karl introduced me to a very tall, thirty-something, friendly man. He said that if I wanted a tour, the caretaker was somewhere in the confines of the walls which surrounded the school and he would open the doors of the schoolrooms. The three of us walked out on the cement balcony, along the enclosed, large square patio around which the school was built. We spotted the old Indian caretaker climbing the steps. He came leisurely ambling toward us as Mr. Kopps called to him. Then Karl and I toured the whole school while the caretaker unlocked and locked the doors as we looked at the modern, picturesque school rooms. I was amazed at how the school was equipped with every modern convenience. There was a science lab, a well stocked library, and a typing room, plus classrooms for kindergarten through the sixth grade.

As we toured the classrooms where Julie and Terry attended school, I felt like we were back in the U. S. A. Their rooms were decorated with pictures of George Washington, for his birthday and hearts for Valentine's day. An oasis in the middle of the desert. It was wonderful to see the American flags and pictures of George and Abraham Lincoln. Karl snapped a picture of me sitting on Julie's desk while George seemed to peek over my shoulder from the wall behind me. What a scene, I thought, realizing I was an incurable American flag waver, now more grateful than ever for my free heritage.

When we arrived home mid-afternoon, we ate the grilled cheese sandwiches Margaret had prepared and then I took a nap which was truly unusual. But even I get exhausted sometimes.

A commodity which we consider indispensable - milk - was only available in Jiddah in cans. Back home, I hadn't even heard of canned milk except for the Carnation and Eagle brands. The fresh-canned milk was imported from Holland. At that very time, the city had run out of all milk. There was none to be bought in the whole city of Jiddah. Leila was the only one in the family who drank milk at all. Fortunately, Margaret kept a good supply on hand and still had some in spite of the shortage.

I found the voice of America on the radio at 2 a.m. They were playing an old once-popular song, *What the World Needs Now is Love, Sweet Love*. The news headline was that the American astronauts from the first sky lab live-in experiment had landed safely back on earth in one of the oceans--I missed the exact one. I suddenly felt like a citizen of the world, not even wondering which ocean. They had broken all records of man's time in space. There was ominous talk of impeaching the American president, Richard Nixon, because of the Watergate scandal. Hard to conceive of it actually becoming a reality.

My seventh film came out of my camera. Karl had been

sending my films out of the country with anyone going to the U.S. They would be mailed to my film developer who would then send them on to my home. I hopefully expected to have many photos developed when I returned. I had bought a new camera just before I left and worried that the once-in-a lifetime pictures would not turn out. Everything in the world was a risk, it seemed, but risks posed such exciting possibilities!

Temperature at this late hour was 75 balmy degrees and air conditioners ran continually. I decided to turn in. Margaret had been sleeping since 10 pm. I could hardly wait to know what tomorrow would bring. Each day got more exciting!

CHAPTER XI

"MALESH" MEANS "WHY BOTHER, WHO CARES?" I DO. OUTSIDE NEWS AND HOME SEEM WORLDS AWAY

The feeling of "malesh" was seeping into my being a little bit by my 11th day in Jeddah. I sunbathed by the deserted pool again at noon today and realized I had begun to like the quiet pervasive peace this land of eternal deserts of time engenders. Just a tiny bit, I could shrug my shoulders at the no-news days and the unhurried pace of Arabia. Contrarily, I felt impatient at how fast the days were going. I had to begin to compress the remaining time into priorities. It was during the zenith of the day by the quiet, sun-kissed blue pool, surrounded by walls of hot cement that I thought of home.

These were fearful moments, realizing how helpless I was to help them from here. I thought of Mother, 75 years old, still living in our small town of Proctor and how she, at least, would be in contact with my family. I thought of Bob, my older brother, living in Madison, Wisconsin, and two sisters, Barbara in Colorado Springs and Mary, the baby of our family, in Philadelphia. Dad had died a few years ago-- he was proud of his family. "Two kings and three queens--a full house," he always said.

I thought of countless things during these few precious hours I spent by the pool. It had been uncountable months since I had relaxed like that. My life was always too busy, hurried and harried. I had to work outside my home for many years and there was never enough time for real meditation and relaxation. I regularly took courses in college and was a part-time writer/historian. I thought of God and my relationship to Him and how I had found that life without the Lord was no life at all. We learned from our Baltimore catechisms in our younger days that "God made us to know Him, to love Him and to serve Him in this world and to be happy with Him in the next." How simple it all sounded--how complicated those memorized words became before I found them to be unquestionably true. How many deeds over the years and flounderings of my spirit had transpired before the words and the belief had become one.

I could go on ad infinitum in this vein about everything I thought about, prayed for and meditated on, but I had to get on with the actual exciting happenings during the days and nights in Arabia.

That evening Jan Copeland took us out for supper to a hotel called the Kureesh Palace. Chris Speake, Karl, Margaret, Jan and I all walked into the large edifice built around an open courtyard. A large fountain and birdbath dominated the middle of this open ceiling area. Even in the dusk, the birds were singing and swooping down to land briefly on the marble floors and skim across the birdbath. We took pictures of us all sitting on the edge of the birdbath.

As we entered the elegant restaurant, we were ceremoniously conducted to a round table with a white linen tablecloth. Waiters in white turbans and green sashes circling their waists, bowed and seated us. Giant fans hanging from the ceilings whirred and stirred the air. It seemed very Casablanca-like, as in the movies, an atmosphere I hadn't previously encountered here in Jiddah. A British atmosphere, even though the menu was written in French and Arabic.

First Jan ordered a bottle of mineral water. Of course we dared not drink water that wasn't boiled. The others ordered for me, because not only was the menu in a foreign language, but I had never heard of the food. Of course when the waiter brought the tossed salad, we left it untouched because the lettuce had not been cloroxed and scrubbed. The meal itself was another new taste experience. I didn't know the names of what I was eating, but I tried it all and it all tasted good and was very interesting. Jan was a gracious host. Such a fun evening! Much cameraderie and laughter abounded at our table! We later drove back to the compound and drank sidiki to finish off the evening.

CHAPTER XII

CHRISTIAN PRAYER GROUP, PERSIAN RUGS AND STREET OF GOLD

Monday, Margaret again escorted me via taxicab to Mia's Beauty Parlor. She and Leila turned around and returned home again in the same cab. Mia's was a beehive of activity and gossip. American women from the different compounds in the city met there and compared notes. It was the true newsroom of Jiddah, and I could see how getting your hair "done" could become an addiction, if for no other reason than to hear the news. Just as in the old days of our western civilization when men met in the pubs or saloons to hear the latest news, here in the city of Jiddah or "Grandmother" the women gathered in an illegal beauty parlor to glean the kernels of news in the city.

Later, prior to a dinner engagement with Chris Speake, Karl and I took a late afternoon trip to the suk. The sun was setting when we arrived about 5:30. The suk was sparkling with lights and very colorful. The aisles were wide and the booths painted with bright paint. I thought it was the most exciting place in the world. One could spend days and weeks in the suk and still not exhaust its possibilities. That evening Karl wanted to take me to see a man who billed himself as "the man from India". His booth, filled with every kind of gleaming brass object, was lit up like a carnival. The brass in the market was often dull but this man's was bright and shiny. He was friendly and talkative and proved himself to be not only a charmer, but a super salesman. I bought some brass camels, a mortar and pestil used to grind spices, a brass coffeepot and some other souvenirs.

Karl also showed me some of the many Persian rug shops, where prices were cheap compared to those in America. The beauty of the oriental rugs was indescribable. If I had any money at all, I would have found it worth the import tax to send one home as a valuable investment, but unfortunately I couldn't afford that luxury.

We had to hurry out of the suk because we had promised to meet Chris, Jan and Margaret at 8 o'clock. Enroute we stopped at the candy booth which was literally filled with every kind of candy and nuts from all over the eastern world. After spending 15 minutes of precious time in deciding, we finally bought some Syrian candy (individually wrapped) and a pound of warm, luscious pistaschio nuts. Again I found that whenever I was in the suk, it was difficult to tear myself away from its insidious and alluring charm.

We hurried out of there and arrived, breathless and a bit late, at the Halowani Hotel. The three others were already there, but so deep in conversation, they hadn't noticed our tardiness. That meal was an adventure in Arabian food. With the help of all those present, I ordered shish kabob, Arabian bread and homos (humas), and different kinds of vegetables that were surprise taste treats. The waiter let me take a menu when we left. Another fun evening! Chris was the hostess and paid the bill--what nice friends Karl and Margaret had.

A tall blonde neighbor named Barbara Henson took me with her to the suk the next afternoon. I knew that Margaret needed a respite from company. I had accepted Barbara's invitation without hesitation, having met her twice before. She and three other women had sent an invitation one day to come to a Bible study group in her home. I had gone, but Margaret didn't. Most of the ladies present were American Southern Baptists, which was fine, but I didn't feel qualified to enter their discussion. Our viewpoints were just different. But it was great to know that some attempts were still being made to retain Christianity in this Moslem land where Christians were considered infidels.

Margaret later told me that for many years Barbara and her husband had been real "party people", seeking worldly pleasures in any shape or form. About a year before, they had had a religious experience or conversion and had done a 90-degree turn-around in their attitude and life style.

Barbara and I took a taxi to the suk to pick up the galibeas for myself and my daughter, Anne. They were ready, I paid for them and it was with excited anticipation that I carried them out of the little shop.

Wandering through the streets or side aisles of the suk, Barbara very quietly whispered that most people laughed when she told them she was reading a book by Pat Boone. "But I just love it," she continued to whisper, "and I found it most enlightening." When I told her I belonged to a charismatic prayer group back home, she was astonished and seemed elated about it. We dropped the subject and continued to buy souvenirs to bring home to America.

But that wasn't the end of it. In the evening Barbara came over to talk with me. She spoke softly and asked if I would meet with her and four other women at her neighbor, Carol's, and teach them how to conduct a prayer meeting.

"What?" I blurted out. I didn't know how to teach anyone, nor did I feel like a qualified leader, but I also knew that the Holy Spirit will blow where He will. So I agreed to meet with them in the morning.

Karl and I were alone in the kitchen when he sat down to talk to me. "Margaret and I have decided to give you a going away present," he said. I listened wondering what he was going to say next. A present? Hadn't they given me presents enough?

I waited, puzzled. He went on. "We're going to give you airfare to go to Jerusalem." I just looked at him, speechless and in disbelief. Tears sprang to my eyes. I reached out to touch his wonderful freckled arm. My God, Jerusalem!

"Please , Karl," I finally spoke, "lend me the money. That will be wonderful enough."

"We're giving it to you for a present," he said. Tears bubbled in my eyes--my throat constricted--I was completely overwhelmed. I could only grab his hand and look at him in gratitude.

"I will see what I can find out about your getting there," he said. "I think you may have to fly to Athens and then back to Tel Aviv. It's far out of the way, but there's no way to get to Israel from here--and you absolutely can't mention it to anyone or we'll all get in trouble!" He was deadly serious. "I'll see if I can get your ticket rewritten, so you can go to Athens and then buy your ticket to Israel from there."

It sounded complicated, being the small town person that I was, but I didn't care. I was so excited. I could go to Jerusalem after all. What may seem impossible, is not when the Holy Spirit gets working on it! I hugged my tall younger brother, whom I had helped nurture during his adolescent days when he and his friends used my home as their hangout. Karl was 9 years younger than I and I was already married and had a daughter when he was still in grade school. I didn't know how to express my appreciation.

Later I walked over to the movie area where the Follies were in rehearsal as they were nightly. The big night was getting close and anticipation completely dominated all of the westerners in the whole city. They were so excited about it, with the opening only a week away on February 21.

I sat in the back of the dark outdoor theatre again. The moon was full and so very low I could almost touch it. The stars were like a low roof over the theatre. As I watched the rehearsal, seeing Karl getting his time-machine into operation, I would have loved to have been able to stay and see how it all looked on the two big nights. But now, if I was going to the Holy City, I would have to leave on Monday the 18th, less than a week away. I could only spend two days there, but it would be two days more than no days. Like this trip, I had no way to map out an itinerary because no one from Arabia could go to a Jewish country. This was the law. Once you had been to Israel, you could not return to an Arabian country.

I loved sitting there in the dark thinking about the letter I had received from home today. It was very welcome. The two Johns said they were getting along all right. It sounded quite heroic, which neither of them were. Big John apparently washes clothes a lot. Grab the brass ring when it comes around was becoming my motto and I had to do what I had to do. I was here and I couldn't let my Freudian guilt ruin the trip. I also got Valentine cards from my friends, Pat, Linda and Betty.

I was listening with interest to Voice of America on the radio. The family was all in bed. Tomorrow would be Wednesday, like Friday to us. It was the end of the working/school week and everyone was tired at the end of the week. The announcer was talking about the energy crisis in America brought about because the Arabs thought we were giving too much aid to Israel. Also, Pulitzer prize winner A. Solzhenitsyn of Russia had been arrested inside his own country because of the book he wrote, *The Gulag Archipelago.*

Thursday we planned to go to the City of Taif. We would have to go around Mecca through the desert. I could hardly wait!

CHAPTER XIII

BEDOUINS/DESERT/ARMED SOLDIERS
ON ROAD TO MECCA

The experience of Thursday, February 14th was, doubtless, one of the unique experiences of my lifetime. I didn't realize what lay ahead that morning when Karl, little Terry, her friend Careme Speake and I drove off onto the road to Taif. Margaret chose not to go with us, a day by herself was a luxury she hadn't enjoyed lately.

Unfortunately, Karl's Toyota began having severe radiator trouble when we were already well out of Jiddah. Karl had brought several large jugs of water and from the time of the first boilover, he had to keep feeding it water every half hour. But it didn't spoil the excitement of driving out into that primitive, unspoiled desert, broken only by the highway on which we sped. It was the only reminder that civilization took this now charted route to Mecca and Taif. Until recently, for countless centuries, the way was known only to the desert-wise Bedouins and the Moslem pilgrims making their way to Mecca.

"Karl, this isn't a sand desert--it has that tall thin grass growing from it, like the downy hair on a person's arm. And look at those hills--they're black and rise so abruptly from the flat land. It's not what I expected at all, more like the background of a nightmare."

"Hey, look, there's a Bedouin camp over there," Karl said excitedly, and I quickly looked through my binoculars to bring closer the three black tents pitched far off the road. I could see little figures moving about. Then we passed a flock of goats milling about and grazing on that thin grass - they were close to the road. Imagine my surprise to see a black-veiled figure, staff in hand, guarding the herd.

As if reading my mind, Karl nodded, "Yes, that's a woman herder and she has to be veiled even out here in the hot sun."

"My God," I gasped, remembering that Sharon Flannagan

had said women were masked or veiled. To see that woman out there in that empty land, completely covered from head to foot in case some man should come along and gaze upon her face, appalled me no end. Perhaps she would never have the chance to know a different kind of life and maybe she was content to be what she was, but I felt sorry and ashamed that some of us in this world, so privileged and free, were still often discontent with our lot--always wanting more! I kept looking back for a long way wondering what it would be like to be in her place, but grateful that I wasn't.

The radiator was steaming again and as we stopped to fill it, we found we were close to a broken down little fort close to the road, on one of the high hillocks. The kids piled out of the car first and scrambled up to the decaying rock structure while I followed close behind. From there we could see many miles in all directions. The fort was built neck high in a circle of stones. Shades of archeology! I picked up a piece of skeleton, some kind of long jawbone with the teeth intact. Karl said it must be the bones of some kind of animal. Little six-year-old Careme and I both wanted it. He was strong-minded and was insisting on having it. In the end, we each took half of it. What a find we had come up with, I thought. Perhaps it was some pre-historic animal--I could envision the archeology professors at the University of Minnesota, where I worked, thinking this was the great find of the century--from the semi-desert of Arabia! It might put the Dead Sea Scrolls to shame, I speculated further, as we took pictures of each other in the fort. Karl conjectured that the primitive rock fort was probably a remnant left from the hundreds of years Arabia was dominated and controlled by the Turks.

Further on down that long, black road, Karl unexpectedly stomped on the brakes, bringing the car to a screeching halt. We all bounced forward, the kids screamed, but we forgave him when we saw a small herd of camels about 200 feet off the road.

"Karl, real dromedary camels!" I said excitedly. We all ran across the warm desert land as a wizened, leather-skinned old Bedouin walked away from his camels in the opposite direction, not casting a backward glance at us, the intruders. There were six camels, three large and three small. The most surprising sight was that old camel herder carrying one of those long nosed brass coffee pots as he walked away. Karl managed to shout to him in lame Arabic, "Can we take pictures of the camels?"

The old man turned and shouted his Arabic, "Yes"-- then asked, "Do you have any riyals?"

"No," Karl shouted back, then laughed his great booming laugh and shook his sandy head. "Even out here they want money," he said. The old man soon disappeared and we never saw him again. The puzzle was that you just can't disappear so quickly in a desert, but he did. He was already gone by the time we chased the camels around the trees they were eating, to get a picture of one of them with me. One camel, who smelled like he needed a dentist for abscessed teeth, kept moving around the tree away from me. He growled and scared me, and I finally gave up the ring-around-the rosy game. Karl took my picture alongside the camel-eaten bush with the camels in the background. Oh well! We did manage to photograph those three babies who all trailed after one mother, although we doubted one camel's ability to give birth to triplets.

We ran back to the car then and drove off down the road after giving the radiator an ample swig of life-reviving water. We were looking for the old camel herder, when Karl startled us by braking to pick up a turbanned Bedouin hitchihiker whom we at first thought must be the owner of "our camels". He was a handsome young man with bright brown eyes and beautiful white teeth that would have enhanced an Ipana toothpaste ad. He climbed into the back seat, exuding excitement about being alive. He flashed his marvelous piano toothed smile often. Karl, who had studied Arabic for a short while, asked him if he owned any camels. He proudly proclaimed that he owned three of them. I fervently wished I could talk with him, his presence in that little car was electrifying. Again, the language barrier kept human beings from communicating effectively.

HANDSOME BEDOUIN HITCHHIKER KARL PICKED UP IN DESERT

KISSING CAMELS IN THE DESERT JUST OFF ROAD TO TAIF

THE KAABA IN MECCA BELIEVED BY MOSLEMS TO HAVE BEEN
BUILT BY ABRAHAM AND HIS SON ISAAC

SMALL ENCAMPMENT OF DESERT WANDERERS

Looking through my binoculars at the desert, I suddenly had an interesting idea. I handed our new friend the glasses. He put them to his eyes and exclaimed in Arabic, "Picture, picture!" Karl caught the implication. The young man had seen a camera before, but now he saw through two eyes and thought it was like a double camera. Made sense to me.

He indicated he wanted to get out near a small encampment off the road. Karl stopped the car and as the hitchhiker squeezed out of the back seat, he smiled at us, his teeth as white and gleaming as pearls, his dark lively eyes dancing as he leaned down to wave goodby outside the car window. I snapped his picture. "My, he's hand-some," I said to Karl as we sped away down the long black-topped ribbon of road.

Karl poured another shot of water into the radiator while the two kids ran across the desert. Careme was brandishing a life-like gun, prompting Karl to shout at him in alarm. "Put that gun away, Careme! If anyone saw that, they might take it for real and we'd all be in touble", although there certainly didn't seem to be anyone for miles around. In fact, it was so very quiet out here in this dry land where St. Paul may have spent the three agonizing years before he set out on his public ministry.

As we skimmed along, a guard station loomed into view. "Oh, oh," Karl said. "We're at the Mecca bypass road. Look in the glove compartment and find Terry's and my passports. Also get yours out." He turned around and asked, "Careme, did you bring yours along?" Six year old Careme handed his to Karl. "They look at everybody's," Karl said. Two guards were running out of their small station toward our car. One came to me with his hand extended and an ominous look in his eyes. I handed him my passport and visa. The guard on Karl's side then came around to my side. They took all four visas and retreated into their guard house to review them and consult about them.

"Mecca is eight miles from here," Karl almost whispered as we waited in nervous anticipation. "This is the closest a non-Moslem can ever get to their holy city." Finally, after an interminable time, the guards ran out and returned our passports, while directing us to take the road to the right, i.e., the bypass road. It seemed like a super turnaround in some fiction fairy tale, almost unbelievable in this enlightened twentieth century. I actually pinched myself as I fearfully peered over my shoulder and saw those armed guards glaring down the road at us as if suspecting we might double back and sneak onto the forbidden Mecca road.

As we drove along, Karl related some tales about Mecca that I had never heard before. In fact, I hadn't realized that when we facetiously said, "Bow to the east", back home, the expression came from the fact that no matter where a Moslem lives in the world, he must bow toward Mecca as he prays five times a day. And usually Mecca is east of wherever they are. The Kaaba, a huge black cube shrine, the "holy of holies" to the Moslems, is in ancient Mecca.

Karl's story was so interesting that I wrote it down in the jolting little car. Here it is: The Kaaba means cube in Arabic and looks like a giant cube. It is 50 feet high, enshrouded in black silk which is inscribed with beautifully embroidered Arabic writings. According to tradition, the sacred black stone in one corner was put there by their prophet and founder, Mohammed.

Historically, the Kaaba is believed to have been built by the ancient prophet, Abraham, and his illegitimate, but first son, Ishmael. Hagar, the servant girl of Sara and Abraham, became the mother of Abraham's son, Ishmael, after Sara laughed when God told her that Abraham would have descendents as numerous as the sands in the desert and that she, Sara would bear a son. In spite ot her sarcasm, Sarah did bear her husband Abraham a son whose name was Isaac. Sara, jealous of Hagar, sent the servant girl and Ishmael away, banishing them out into the barren uninhabited desert. (To me this was enlightening as to how the ancient patriarchs lived. Abraham was also just a nomad as the wandering tribes are today).

Hagar and her child, Ishmael, wandered in the desert until her child was about to perish from thirst. There, in the place where Mecca was later founded, she prayed for water and then thought she saw water on the next knoll. Running over there, she was bitterly disappointed to find it was an optical illusion. She then thought she saw water from the place she had just come. She ran back again, carrying her child. Six times she was disappointed. But, the seventh time she ran back to the other knoll, a miraculous spring of fresh water was shooting out of the ground. Gratefully she gave her son and herself water to drink which saved their lives. The ritual is still commemorated to this day. The Moslems run between the knolls seven times during their yearly holy days of Ramadan. The well of Hagar still gives abundant water and is called the well of Zam Zam. It runs between the Safa and Al-Marwah hills. When Abraham rode out to the place called Mecca to see his son, Ishmael, he promised Sara he wouldn't get off his horse while visiting Hagar and his first born son. Legend says he visited his son in this manner for many years.

Later, when Ishmael grew up, God commanded Abraham and Ishmael to build a temple near that very well, which they did. Today, the stone they stood on while building the Kaaba, is loved and revered by the Moslems.

The Moslems are of the Islamic religion. They believe it was Ishmael who God asked Abraham to sacrifice, because Ishmael was the oldest son. But the Israelites dispute this because it is written in the Old Testament that it was Isaac, the legitimate son, who God asked Abraham to sacrifice. However, the Moslems believe that the Kaaba in Mecca was the altar of the sacrifice where God stopped Abraham from sacrificing his son to prove his obedience to His command.

Every Moslem must visit Holy Mecca at least once in his lifetime in order to fulfill his religious obligation. Each year during the month of "Ramadan", or the "Pilgrimage", over a million pilgrims or Hajii (hagees) as they are called, pour into the Red Seaport of Jiddah, the nearest debarcation point to Mecca. They come by land, sea and air from all over the world. It is a colorful spectacle for the non-Moslem to see, and a most meaningful pilgrimage to those who make it -- the greatest trip of their lifetime. The Moslems make up one sixteenth of the world's population.

By this time we could see the mountain ahead of us. Karl said we had to drive to the top of it. It looked formidible and seemed much closer than it was. We could see it for many miles as we approached it. Other than stopping now and then to fill the radiator, from here to the mountain was uneventful as we skimmed along the desert road. Then out of nowhere loomed a shacky little store built at the foot of the mountain. It was almost like a tent, but built of some kind of wood, along with some tarp or what have you. Karl stopped the car and said I couldn't go in because women were not allowed in a public place in the desert. At first I thought he was kidding, the only place we had seen for 100 miles, but he was dead serious. He went in to buy some cold pop. The kids and I didn't even dare stretch our legs because we could see some old men sitting in an open-air type coffee shop in the back, drinking their coffee. They sat cross-legged and stared at us with dark piercing eyes. Across the road we saw a huge herd of goats and a veiled woman tending then.

The sun beat down unmercifully now. We were tired and dreadfully thirsty. I thought how typical it was here for the men to be drinking coffee like they had nothing else to do and the lonely woman across the road couldn't go inside, nor did she apparently deserve any refreshment. Karl came back to the car carrying Pepsi-Cola bottles. What a surprise, in this land of awesome contrasts! Pepsi-Cola out in this shack in the lonely desert? I shook my head and enjoyed drinking it although it wasn't very cold!

Now we were on the mountain road heading up, 54 miles to the top with an average of six turns to the mile. As we wound further and further up, the view became more long range and exciting. There were many contrasting hues of different colors. Around and around, up and up, as we continually looked far down at the narrow road twisting like a snake as it would up the mountain. We passed a few houses/cabins/camps along the way. They were set right smack against the side of the mountain. It reminded me a little bit of some of the houses perched on the hillside of Duluth, which is the large city of 100,000 adjacent to our

KARL, CAREME SPEAKE AND TERRY POSE BESIDE AN OLD
TURKISH FORT ON ROAD TO ANCIENT TAIF ON THE MOUNTAIN

AMAZING WINDING ROAD, ENGINEERED BY BEN LADEN
(LAHDEN) ACROSS THE MOUNTAINS TO TAIF

TWO OLD ARABS DRINKING COFFEE IN THE AFTERNOON SUN

PILGRIMS ON THEIR WAY TO MECCA

home town of Proctor, a city of 3,000 population. I thought how these Arabians would have loved to gaze upon the largest of the Great Lakes, Lake Superior, instead of the dry waterless desert.

The road was an engineering accomplishment of great magnitude built by Ben Laden (Lahden), who had never attended engineering school, but was known for his ingenious engineering feats all over the Mideast. Karl explained this to me as he diligently followed the road, winding, winding, narrow, the sides dropping off into eternity. Finally arriving at the top, almost dizzy from the winding ascent, we stood on top of the mountain. I was glad to stretch my legs. We gazed in fascination at the far vistas of the unending desert, also other mountain ranges. We could see all the way down to the bottom of the spiral road we had driven. I took pictures of this unusual view and then Karl set the nose of our little car toward Taif, which he said was still 25 miles cross country once we had reached the top which leveled off on a plateau.

Terry and Careme were giggling and singing in the back seat as we drove the last lap of our journey to the city which, Karl guessed, might have a population of 40,000 people, but, he admitted, it was an uneducated estimate because there was no way to count people in Saudi Arabia today.

"Why not?" I asked.

"How would you count people if there weren't any taxes, nor voting, nor registering for anything? They wouldn't know where to begin taking a census. They're still too close to being a nation of Bedouins." Karl shrugged. "Even if a person rents a house, only the owner of house is registered and often there aren't any street names. If there's a telephone in your rented house, it is listed only in the name of the owner so you couldn't find a person's telephone number unless you knew who owned the house."

"Karl, you must be kidding. You mean they actually run a country like that?"

He nodded, as the city of Taif suddenly loomed out of the desert. Even on top of the mountain as the road evened out, the country had become desolate wasteland until there was a city in front of us, like a mirage. As we drove into the ancient metropolis, I could see evidence of the hundreds of years of Turkish domination. A walled fort, about two blocks square, massive and impressive, was our first view of Taif.

"Remember hearing about Lawrence of Arabia, Claire?" Karl asked, while he admonished the kids, Terry and Careme, not to make so much noise. We couldn't talk above the din as they continued to sing and giggle in the back seat. I nodded hesitantly. I didn't know much about Lawrence.

"The Arabians were in bondage to the Turks for hundreds of years. Or maybe not exactly in bondage, but the Turks had conquered Arabia, when this British army man, Lawrence, who loved this part of the world, urged the Arabians to unite and chase the Turks out of here. He rode through the desert talking to the Bedouins until he got these people from all the far flung parts of Arabia to band together. To make a long story short, they drove the Turks out under Lawrence's leadership. You must read *Lawrence of Arabia* by Lowell Thomas. I have it at home--it's fascinating how Lawrence managed to unite these independent tribes. who felt no allegiance to each other.

"I don't see how that was possible, Karl," I exclaimed. "A foreigner coming here -- an Englishman at that -- gaining the trust of these primitive people, especially the desert dwellers? How did he do it?" Even as I asked, I was watching where we were driving and I noticed the people looked much the same as in Jiddah, large swarthy men, sitting in their outdoor coffee houses or strolling along the street holding hands. The city of Taif itself, had a different flavor or feeling about it. Jiddah was a seaport with the environment that went with it and this city was isolated atop a mountain, far from any other place. There was an inexplicable difference.

"It happened in about 1922 when Abdul Aziz, who was King Faisal's father, rode at the head of the united Arabians and regained control of their land again," Karl was still speaking of the Lawrence of Arabia era. "Abdul Aziz became their King even though he himself was a Bedouin

King, still fresh from the desert. Lawrence managed to unite them and King Abdul Aziz led the revolt against the Turks.

"What amazes me," I said, "is that Abdul Aziz was almost like Abraham, a wandering desert patriarch, probably living under the same conditions as Abraham, thousands of years ago, when he became head of his tribe. I can hardly believe I'm going through this, Karl. Thanks for making this journey possible and I patted his strong capable hand and wondered how his tall frame could ride so long in that compact car. He was so knowledgeable and generous about sharing it all. I remembered when Karl taught in Nome, Alaska, and when he came home, he showed us slides. Our family felt almost as though we had been there ourselves. It was the same when he spent two years in the Peace Corps in the West Cameroons in Africa. That's when he and Margaret met. They both taught English in the Peace Corps and Margaret also was from the State of Minnesota. They were married in the Cameroons.

We stopped beside a building that was being rennovated. It was surrounded by scaffolding covered with tarp. To shield the workers from the sun, I guessed, although few workers were seen now, because it was already 2 p.m., siesta time. It was a white stucco hotel and Karl speculated that this hotel was apparently being added to, or subtracted from. We walked in through narrow walkways and ramps. Once inside, we were in a cool marble hallway lined with portraits of King Faisal and some of his sons. From there, we were ushered into a cool, pleasant dining room, unexpectedly elegant in this place. "Many of the very rich Arabians, have summer homes up here in the mountains; that is, if they don't have a villa on the Red Sea," Karl explained, as the turbanned waiter led us to an oblong table set with linens, white plates and all the silverware settings, (with buzzing fans and much cool marble in the room). He bowed and spoke to us in English. The atmosphere breathed British, a complete contrast to the sun-drenched desert and hot little car that we had spent more time in than we had anticipated, because of the leaky radiator.

The bowing waiter first brought us a minced pie (pastry filled with meat and topped with onions). Next we were treated to some exotic foods. Batter-dipped french fried cauliflower. Delicious! Buttered carrots and scallops (which was really breaded veal) and a lot of other new taste treats. I love to eat, but now I wish I had been more observant and/or asked someone what went into these marvelous dishes. We, of course enjoyed the ever present Arabian bread and homos to dunk it in. After about five different courses the polite, bowing waiter brought some of the marvelous out-of-this-world backlava for dessert. It is a baked dough that has many, many thin layers of delicious nutmeats rolled into it -- so thin that it is rolled many times, then cut and baked. Sinfully luscious! We were served an apple, as the last course, to finish off the meal. Our appetites were wonderfully appeased.

CHAPTER XIV

THE WRIGHTS/NIGHT IN DESERT/ARABIANPARTY

From the hotel, we set off to find Karl's friends, the Wrights. Mr. Wright was a former English teacher in Jiddah, but now was superintendent of the "western school" here in Taif. How would we find them. There were few street names, telephones only in the names of the owners and certainly no tourist bureau.

There wasn't one human being in sight as we drove along the narrow rutted path that substituted for a road. Karl pounded on the door of the first house we saw. The door opened furtively. Karl began to ask directions in his limited Arabic. He valiantly attempted to explain who we were looking for to the man who answered the door -- the man didn't comprehend. Karl then tried to explain Mr. Wright's position. The man gave some instructions in Arabic which Karl tried to follow, but again we were hopelessly lost -- more inquiries -- more lost. But inch by inch we were getting closer. I marveled at Karl's infinite patience. I remembered when he was my small kid brother, he threw terrible tantrums when he didn't get his way. Apparently he had come a long way since then -- literally and figuratively.

After about an hour or more, we did arrive at the house of the Wrights. When I think about it, it was nothing short of the marvel of the ages that we found it at all. We knocked at the gate and it was opened by smiling Mary Ann Wright, an attractive lady in her mid-thirties, who was delighted to see her old friend, Karl. Karl introduced us and explained that Margaret had elected to stay home with baby Leila and Julie. Mary Ann said that her husband had left for the states the previous day. She invited us in. Their villa was different than those I had seen in Jiddah. Even though walled in, as every place in Arabia was, there the similarity seemed to end. Their villa was located at the base of a mountainous hill. The so-called basement was on the ground level. Mary Ann gave us the grand tour. First floor had a game room, a bedroom and bath. We walked a few steps up to the roomy main floor, which included the huge master bedroom, living room, spacious hallway, two other bedrooms, large kitchen and dining room. Then another floor--that too was roomy and bright. We climbed more stairs to the roof, flat but with a marvelous view of the city, the mountain and the desert. We stood there and looked at the panoramic view. It was too flat and treeless for me to admire it, but it was so different from the hilly city I was from. In the neighbor's yard, chickens and goats were scavenging the garbage. We watched three ladies, veiled from head to toe, scurry across the street. A goat herder was herding his goats past the mosque. The hour of prayer was at hand. The muezzin or caller was shouting the prayer call from his tower. His voice sounded strange and flat to my ears.

In the distance we could see the suk. Friendly Mary Ann explained all the sights. "The kids love to climb this mountain behind our house. We throw the garbage outside -- we did quit once but our neighbors complained that their chickens didn't have enough to eat, so now we throw it out again just like everyone else.

"That's the kind of garbage collecting we need back home," I chuckled. She laughed. She appraised me then. "Your sister is pretty," she said to Karl. "You both are fair skinned, but she is not covered with freckles as you are. She has reddish hair, but yours is darker." It was like I wasn't standing right there. "She is much more smiley than you, although you have such a hearty laugh and good sense of humor, Karl." Then she turned to me. "Do you share that humor in your family?"

I looked at Karl and laughed. "We think we have a great sense of humor. You should have seen us five kids and my mom and dad at the dinner table when we were growing up. We all contributed to the conversation and quips were flying like lightning. Then little fat Karl would get a laughing fit and he would go into gales and gales of laughter 'til we all laughed until we had tears in our eyes. Someone would say, 'What are we laughing at?' and no one knew."

"You mean Karl was ever fat?" I smiled and glanced at

Karl. "He was the short, pudgy one that we thought was going to be short -- instead...". I laughed and looked up at him from my 5 ft. 5 in position. We went downstairs for coffee then and later when the sun was about to disappear over the distant horizon, we left the Wright home and drove off toward the suk. Karl let Terry, Careme and me off to shop for a bit while he took his car to a garage hoping they could clean out his radiator which continued to be an infuriating problem today. It had spoiled much of the day because we continually had to fill that boiling radiator! The kids and I walked into the market place. Every city has its own special kind of suk. I didn't dare walk very far into it because I feared I might never find the entrance again and maybe no one spoke English. I kept my eye on the entryway through the maze of booths and stores. The lights were coming on and I didn't buy anything there. We had agreed to meet Karl in half an hour and we met at the entrance to the suk. The garage man had flushed out the radiator, hopeful that would fix it. We hurried to get out of Taif now. It had been an interesting time up here, but barely long enough to capture the flavor of the ancient city on the mountain, fortressed by Turkish strongholds and architecture. We were driving as fast as possible to get to and down the mountain before dusk turned to black night. The sun was already about to drop, which it seemed to do without a sunset as if disappearing forever. It was almost dark when we reached the top of the mountain road with its many curves and craggy peaks looming in front of us. Down we headed though, as had the sun and it wasn't long before the little Toyota was turning and twisting in the dark silence of ancient Saudi Arabia. There were no lights, nor cars. The temperature gauge started to rise again about halfway down the Ben Laden mountain road. We watched that gauge in alarm praying it wouldn't boil over before we got to the desert floor.

I didn't even get Margaret a valentine!" blurted out of the darkness as Karl suddenly realized what day it was. The car trouble had driven almost everything else from our thoughts. Terry and Careme had quieted down in the back now, tired from the long day's adventures. Karl and I talked about

Mother and Dad's wedding anniversary on Valentine's Day. Dad had died a few years ago, but Mother always said she felt like it was their day, so she never thought to give valentines to anybody else.

"I wonder what she did today?" I asked. But Karl reminded me that it was probably only about noon back home. "Maybe brother Bob and sisters Mary and Barb will call her," I said. "Maybe there's a snowstorm," I further speculated, happy that it was so lovely and balmy here, although the desert air was cool.

At last, through a tense couple of hours, we breathed a bit easier as we reached the base of the mountain. We sped along the narrow road in the darkest night I have ever witnessed. It was as if we were the only people alive in the world, although the stars seemed more numerous than the sands of the desert.

What was exciting was to glimpse tiny bonfires back in the desert. When we stopped to water the radiator, I stood out under that glorious ebony sky and listened to the bark of a Bedouin's dog mixed with far-away voices, while the surrounding silence was so vast that it was as if we had wandered into eternity. "I can't believe this," I said to the blackness of the night. Everything was terribly new and exciting in this ancient land and that seemed paradoxical. We had to go, although it would have been marvelous to stay awhile. I did wonder what secrets the desert was hiding. The thought of rattlesnakes and other crawly things came to mind, only to be dispelled by the wonder of it all. No wonder Paul went into the desert of Arabia for three years before starting his ministry to the gentiles. It is said that only here one can really feel and know God. I can understand that now, although how I would do after about two days is hard to know.

We had been invited to an Arabian party that evening--at 8:30. It was that time now. "I suppose Margaret's going to be really mad at us," Karl said, "even if we couldn't help it." Now we were at the turn of the Mecca cutoff. No one stopped us this time, as we turned in the direction away from Mecca.

"I once heard of a man who accidentally missed the turnoff to the bypass road. I don't know where the guards were, but like tonight it would be easy to turn the wrong direction. When he found himself in a city, he thought it was Jiddah and he wasn't too alarmed when a policeman stopped him and ordered him to show his papers. Surprised, he found he had accidentally driven to Mecca. That was quite an error."

"Did you ever hear what happened to him?"

"He was immediately deported out of the country."

"I suppose he had to feel lucky to get out alive," I said facetiously. We again caught the light of the occasional bonfire against the sky as we sped through the desert on this memorable night. I'll never forget that feeling of eternity nor how many more stars there seemed to be in that ancient sky -- so low it almost merged with the desert. It was almost like a solid roof over our heads. Karl and Margaret opened a door for me when they brought me here, that I could never have dreamed of otherwise.

At ten we arrived home -- very tired. Margaret was unhappy and impatient and had decided to go bed in spite of being dressed up for the party. Karl and I hurriedly changed our clothes and managed to talk her into going to Samir Akari's party for a awhile at least.

CHAPTER XV

AN ARABIAN PARTY/BELLYDANCING/EXOTIC FOOD/ A PALESTINIAN'S STORY

Karl and I were almost too tired to go to a party after the long trip to and from Taif. Margaret was ready to turn in for the night when we finally got back. Even though the garage in Taif purportedly repaired the radiator, we had to stop often in the dark desert to fill it up when it became too hot. Nevertheless, Julie and Samir were giving this party in honor of my visit, so we quickly freshened up, changed clothes and within half an hour were on our way to the Akari's villa.

I had met Samir (Sameer) one day when Karl showed me his school. There are six English teachers employed to teach the English language by rote to the Saudi airline employees. Four men were American, one a Palestinian and I think Samir may have been Lebanese. He was very friendly and handsome. He and Karl, having worked together over the years, were on very friendly terms. I had heard both Margaret and Karl speak of him and his wife, Julie. After that day, Samir talked with Julie and they decided to show me, as Karl's sister, what the night life of Jiddah was like.

On the way to the Akari's, Margaret explained that Julie was also an English teacher as was Samir. In fact, she was a professor at Dar-Al-Tarbia College, the only women's college in Arabia, which was just three years old.

We stood outside the wall in a narrow alleyway for at least five minutes after we rang the bell before Samir opened the gate. He escorted us into his villa through a long hallway. On the right we passed a little nook where Samir's small office was. We could see his desk overflowing with papers. As we passed by, Samir explained that many of the papers were from the school that he and Julie conducted. I didn't understand at the time, but later was told that he and Julie taught English classes in their home.

As we continued down the long narrow hallway, we passed by three mysterious closed doors, before we arrived in a large comfortable living room. An attractive lady in her thirties rose to greet us. It was Julie, surprisingly light complected, whereas Samir was darker, but lighter than Saudi men. Julie said she wasn't a bit put out that we arrived at 10 instead of 8:30. "We are night people here in this land," she said with a genuine smile as she offered me her hand. Others were arriving behind us. Some spoke no English while others were students of the Akari's and spoke limited English. One guest was a Saudi girl who spoke excellent English.

Samia (Sameea)) Al Edrisi, slender with long dark hair was very friendly. It was only later when we sat down that I had the opportunity to talk with her. She said she was one of six daughters of an Arabian Sheik (Shake). She had been sent to Cairo, Egypt, to be educated. While there she became a liberated woman. So much so, that she refused to wear the veil when she returned to Jiddah.

"My father could have turned me away and never accepted me as his daughter again," she explained. "Most men would do that if their daughters didn't live according to the rules of the household. My mother and five sisters all live behind the veil. But my father is quite a progressive man and he did let me come home to live, even though I am an announcer at a radio station here in Jiddah.

"Really?" I could hardly believe my ears. "What kind of business is your father in?" I asked.

"He's a contractor, you know a builder," she explained. Julie told me later they were very rich.

We were also introduced to a dark young man named Mohammed (a name common to many Arabian men) and his beautiful dark haired, but fair skinned wife who was from Syria. The wife then introduced me to her blue-eyed, fair-haired Syrian mother who had recently arrived from Damascus. That plump little mother sat side by side with me on the couch and she and I communicated through her bilingual daughter. I expressed my surprise at an Arab lady being so light with blue eyes. I learned that in Damascus there are blonde and brunette Syrians. Again, I now heard about the plight of the Palestinians. I found that this sweet little lady had fled from Damascus because the Israelis had flown over and bombed the people out of their houses.

"Were they bombing military places or factories?" I asked. All of them looked at me in disgust for asking. Quickly and in unison they shook their heads. "No, they bomb us continually. Haven't you seen the many thousands of refugees living in tents on the side of the road?", the Syrian lady's son-in-law asked.

"No," I admitted, but I showed I was interested in hearing more. He wanted to know what news we heard in America about the fighting between the Israelis and the Palestinians. I told him we were only given the Israeli side of the question. We were told about the acts of terror perpetrated by the Arabs. "The Jews send out constant news stories," I said. "There are none from the Palestinians."

"Don't Americans ever hear about how we are constantly being either bombed out of our homes and even in our camps -- for no reason at all? he asked, his dark eyes intense and angry.

I shook my head. "I had no idea about the Palestinian side until Karl mentioned it to me, "I confessed.

"We are a people without a country. Our homeland has been taken from us. First the Jews were given Tel Aviv and some of our other land by a decree of the western powers. Since then they are constantly taking more and more of our land because they need more room to expand. There are many rich Jews in the United States who pay much money to make them sound as though they have a just cause in taking it away from us." I was taken aback at the thunder in Mohammed's voice as he continued. The room full of people was as silent as a tomb. "They have no just cause -- it isn't right to throw us out and take over our homes!"

I stood in stunned silence, as he turned around and began to speak in his native Arabic to some of the others. I sat down on the couch again beside the Syrian grandma and tried to digest some of this. I remembered the first time I had heard the Palestinian side of things when Karl's family was visiting us back in Proctor, Minnesota in the summer of 1972. Karl, Margaret, my mother and I drove to Madison, Wisconsin for our nephew's wedding, brother Bob's son. I couldn't remember how the subject had come up, but I did remember how Karl and I had "words" over the issue of the Israeli Jews and the Palestinians. After all, I, as every other American at that time, had been exposed only to the Jewish side of the issue. We were led to feel very sorry over the plight of the Jews who had no homeland until they were reunited to their home in Israel as promised in the Bible. We all felt a sense of responsibility for the six million Jews who had been so brutally exterminated in Germany and Poland when no one on the whole earth would take them in. So, to me, it seemed natural and good that they finally had a homeland. Often, the paper would print a news release from Israel about the terrorist activity of the Palestinians that sounded barbaric. When the Jews reported they had bombed a village or a refuge camp in retaliation, no one thought twice about it. I told Karl this, that day, while we sped through the lush picturesque Wisconsin landscape. I remembered now, how angry he had gotten.

"They can't go in there and take it away from the people who live there and who have lived on the land since Biblical times! Don't any of you back here realize there are hundreds of refuge camps full of tents all over the Mideast where the refugees from Jerusalem and the places the Jews have claimed, live or exist? They have been thrown out or bombed out of their homes, in a homeland which historically and biblically, belongs to them just as much as to the Jews. They are also descended from Abraham, through Ishmael, the eldest son, and they believe they are a part of God's promise to Abraham just as surely as the Jews."

The whole concept of the Palestinians having a "just cause" had been new to me that day and I found, as Karl continued to talk about it, that he had Palestinian friends and that he knew first hand what was going on. At that time my mind had changed a bit, suddenly realizing that we, in America, were often being fed propaganda from the Israelis who knew how to influence the news media, while the other side had no voice, nor any leader except the terrorist, Arafat.

"Would you like to meet the Syrian Ambassador?" My reverie had taken me so far away that I didn't hear Mohammed when he first asked me that question.

"The Syrian Ambassador?" I repeated the question.

"Yes, if you would like to, I will arrange it. I'd like you to talk to him," he said earnestly.

"But, I can't do any good," I protested. "I can only try to tell the people what I have seen and heard when I get home."

"Not many can come here, you know," his wife said. "We think anyone who is a writer, as you are, and is interested in our cause can help us."

I realized then, that it was because I was a writer, even though of small repute, that they thought I might be influential. "I'd like to meet him," I said. Mohammed explained he would arrange it and notify Karl when it was time. I thought it all sounded so exciting, but as happened with some other unfinished business, my time had become so short and that situation was pretty "iffy".

Pretty Julie, wearing a long dress, brought dinner in on plates. It was now midnight, but apparently the usual time to serve dinner. The main dish was wonderful barbequed chicken with other tasty foods. One vegetable was a pepper lentil dish made with a form of beanlike vegetable and a salad called Fatoosh which consisted of cress, cucumber, tomatoes and croutons, with a lemony flavor. There were dates to munch on, and Arabian bread to dunk in spinach homos. All of it was well flavored with a variety of fresh herbs and spices.

Samir had turned on the hi-fi which was playing Arabian music. Their music sounded strange to me because it is based on the quarter note instead of the half note as our music is. It seemed to me more like a wail than a melody. As it played, the ladies stood up and tied sashes around their waists, while their torsos began vibrating. They belly-danced exotically in front of me because I had asked them if they would. The men then joined the vibrating women and the whole room was alive with rhythmically swaying belly dancers, artistic and exquisite to watch. I hardly noticed when Karl and Margaret exited. Karl returned soon saying Margaret had been tired and he had driven her home. She was very much a morning person. Midnight was very late to her.

It was about 2:30 a.m. when the other guests said good-night and left. Even though I was almost sleep walking, and Karl must have been the same, we stayed for a last "one for the road" drink. It was a bit of some smooth liquor which may have been smuggled in from Beirut. As Julie, Samir, Karl and I relaxed and visited, I asked Samir what the brass lettering said on a plaque hanging on the wall. "It says 'Ahlan was sahlan' which means 'welcome to our home'." He stood up and removed the brass Arabian lettering off the wall. "I'd like to give it to you to take home in memory of us. Please hang it on your wall." He smiled his charming smile and handed it to me while Julie nodded in concurrence. I accepted it and told them I'd treasure it and hang it in a place of honor in my living room.

"In a few more days, I must return home," I said. Julie asked me if I'd like to go to the Women's University with her. I looked at Karl who said, "Sure, if you want to". Julie said I could go with her the next evening. Karl arranged to bring me back to their home about 4 p.m. I didn't know until then that Julie taught in a women's college in the late afternoon and evening.

"Also, would you like to meet Princess Jahara?"

"Is she a real Princess?" I blurted out.

Julie nodded. I smiled big and said I'd love to. Julie said she'd call Princess Jawhara's secretary to arrange a visit with her. I couldn't wait to see if this would all come about. Finally, lamenting the fact that there weren't 24 waking hours a day, Karl and I thanked the Akari's and I drove home across the City which was quieter now. I was excited about all that was unfolding and could hardly believe this was still a continuation of the day that we had gone to Taif. I realized I would forget in the flurry of tomorrow if I didn't record these incidents that night, as we were scheduled to go to the cabin on the Red Sea the next day.

CHAPTER XVI

TICKY-TACKY CABINS ON THE RED SEA

Margaret and I rode in the front seat with Karl on a long, desert road enroute to the Creek that Friday morning. The Creek is a peninsula that stretches its long arm into the Red Sea. Forty miles from Jiddah someone had built a colony of so called "camps" or "cabins". I had never seen anything as strange as these shack-like cubicles. Only a few of them actually border on the sea while the rest are built behind the front camps. From some of them the sea is hardly visible, but to rent a camp for a year is very expensive. If you consider it's the only beach in the whole area, even "beehives", which these cabins resembled, become valuable commodities. To breathe some fresh air from the Red Sea in this arid land is important. Apparently other shores of the sea do not lend themselves to camps. Even though Jiddah is built along the shore also, it's long and dirty and every kind of sea going vessel from ocean ships to fishing craft are sitting in the harbor.

We had been invited to spend the day with friends, who had rented a cabin in the third row from the sea. Usually three families would share one camp, divide the expenses and take turns vacationing there on weekends. This cabin consisted of a screened porch, a cubbyhole kitchen and a tiny bedroom plus a small indoor toilet; otherwise there was nothing to it. The front cabins were built on tall legs right into the water. I snapped a picture of a bikini-clad American lady sitting on her front steps sunning, while her feet dangled in the cool water. Thelma and Jim were wonderful hosts and we talked and visited in their little screened porch while the kids played in the water. Later, we had good old hot dogs and baked beans for dinner, just like back home. Then, Karl inflated his four-man rubber boat. Karl, Margaret, Terry and myself settled comfortably into it and went chugging out into the bouncing waters of the colorful Red Sea. We couldn't have asked for a more beautiful, sunny day. Putting on Karl's goggles I peered beneath the clear water and saw many different species of fish, including exotically colored goldfish and other tropical undersea treasures.

By evening, we were sunburned and tired. The home trip across the desert seemed very long with six of us cramped in the little compact car. This road didn't have a feeling of the desert as the road to Taif had -- it was more like an endless service road. What really put the finishing touches on the day was the traffic congestion we were involved in when nearing the outskirts of Jiddah. It had been a forty mile trip across the sands and now we found that many other people had spent their weekend (Thursday and Friday) outside the city, also. Many rich Saudis had summer homes on the sea and they seemed to converge on the one road into Jiddah at once. Being caught in Friday night traffic congestion in Jiddah makes an accident on the Los Angeles freeway seem like fun.

As I mentioned before, these Saudi drivers were like kids with a toy, having never learned traffic rules, nor how to behave when being in possession of a possible lethal weapon, like a car. The constant honking by every car owner, total disregard of another's rights, the closed fist of anger from the occupant of one car among a thousand people in a traffic tie up was its own form of hell. Poor Karl, who was already so tired from his involvement in the Follies, his work and his attempts to show me everything, seemed really wonderful not to blow his cool through all this congestion. Margaret and the three kids were all just as tired, but we ultimately made it with no one the worse for wear.

The next morning, Karl, Julie and Terry began another week of work and school, and Margaret, two year old Leila and I settled into our own little routines. I got back to my hour of solitude alongside the swimming pool.

111

MARGARET AND LEILA BOATING ON THE "CREEK". AN INLET
ARM OF THE RED SEA

PINK PALACE OR GUEST VILLA WHERE MONARCHS,
PRESIDENTS AND OTHER LUMINARIES STAY WHEN VISITING
ARABIA

THE OLD
AIRPORT
IN JIDDAH

CHAPTER XVII

WOMEN'S UNIVERSITY IN ARABIA? UNIQUE!

I had no idea what to expect this evening when Karl left me at Julie Akari's villa. Julie met me at the gate wearing an ankle-length dress and looking pretty, with her shoulder length light-brown hair and soft blue eyes. We caught a taxi almost immediately and I was off on a new adventure. As we drove through the horn-tooting traffic, she told me she taught English at the Saudi girls' college during the late afternoon and early evening. It was 4:30 p.m. as we rode along in the taxi. She didn't tell me much more.

"You'll probably think this college is more on a level with an American high school," she said. "Until three years ago, there was no place of higher learning for any Arabian girl."

"Really?" I said, only now realizing that I really hadn't learned very much about the people here, because hardly any of the "westerners" really interacted with the natives. I asked Julie if the girls wore veils inside the school.

She shook her head. "When they are inside the walls, they are unveiled because men are not allowed on the girls' campus. In fact, if the girls ever need to learn a subject from a male professor, it is broadcast over closed circuit TV from the men's college across the street. It is the same with the library. We are just building a library onto the college, but meanwhile the existing library is small and inadequate, so if the girls need to use the other library, they must do it on Thursday when the young men are out of school for the weekend."

I listened with great interest and growing excitement. Soon we were getting out of the taxi right in front of the college wall and we entered through the gate. Inside, I saw a large square building, all on one floor. Much like the PCS school, it was built around a large patio. We entered the building through the patio, which was landscaped with beautiful flowers, shrubs and green grass, a great contrast to the barren sandy street outside the school.

Julie immediately rushed off to teach her English class. But first she introduced me to the secretary of the college, whose name was Samia (Sameea), and told me over her shoulder as she went into her classroom that if I wanted to go home anytime before 8:30, Samia would have one of the school drivers take me home. Then she ran off, her long full skirt swinging around her ankles. I didn't think to ask her why she didn't have to wear a veil on the outside like the others. Perhaps because she was also a foreigner in Arabia. Julie almost looked "western", with her light brown hair and fair complexion, as opposed to the dark-eyed, brunette Arabians.

Samia, the tall thin young secretary, could speak English quite well. While we appraised each other and wondered how to speak, I saw her as dark-haired and serious -- perhaps studious--with her dark-rimmed glasses and uncurled shoulder-length hair.

"I'm a secretary at the University of Minnesota in America," I said, thinking it was something we had in common. But I soon found that we didn't consider our positions similar. Samia almost immediately told me that she had graduated in Business Administration in three years. This was unprecedented because, she said, "Almost always we must go to college five years." Also she had graduated summa cum laude with a B.A. degree, and then because she was the top one in her class, she was chosen to be the one and only secretary for the college. I was dumbfounded at this revelation, because I was only one of many secretaries at our University, which, had an enrollment of 6,000 students. I often felt that my position was more like being a "girl Friday" to the professors. I didn't feel a bit exalted, but then I'm not a college graduate either, although I continually take classes in pursuit of my degree. I didn't explain this to Samia, but let it go at her assumption that she and I were on the same level -- exalted!

Shyly she showed me the diamond ring on her fourth finger. "I just became engaged," she confided softly.

I admired the beautiful diamond and asked her if it was an arranged marriage. "Yes," she replied, "my parents arranged it with his parents."

"Have you met him?" I asked, hardly believing that I posed such a question. It seemed so silly, but it didn't seem so to Samia.

"I have met with him twice," she said. "We walked around the garden together."

"Aren't you frightened to marry a man you hardly know?"

She giggled a bit nervously and said, "Yes, I am".

Already the young ladies were hurrying out of their classrooms from the 50 minute classes. Samia and I were standing in the doorway of her little office. As the students passed by, I saw the faces of Arabian women for the first time since I had arrived three weeks ago. Some were very pretty, others plain looking. Most of them had straight dark hair because they were not allowed to curl it. A few had naturally curly black hair. They eyed me with their brown eyes, not accustomed to strangers in the school, just as curiously as I watched them. Some of them returned my smile.

My guide said she'd give me a tour of the school. First we went into the library, a small, single room, with only a fraction of the books we might enjoy in a small town high school -- inadequate for a college. I asked Samia how many major fields they could choose from to get a degree.

"We have only five different divisions," she said. "Whichever one we choose, we must attend all the classes that go with it. If I take Business Administration, then for five years, all the classes in that field are required."

They had no choice of subjects then, I realized. "Our first year here is spent getting used to the school -- getting oriented," she said.

Samia then knocked on one of the classroom doors and a lady professor came to the door. Samia explained who I was. The professor greeted me graciously, immediately asking if I'd "talk" to her drama class. I swallowed. I was not prepared nor accustomed to speaking before a class, but then I told myself that I could field their questions because none of them knew anything about America and I was the only authority around at that moment. I agreed and Samia left me with the lady professor to return to her office.

Suddenly I was standing in front of twenty young ladies. I hadn't caught the teacher's name, but she told them that I would tell them who I was, so she hadn't caught mine, either. I pronounced my name, Claire Schumacher, which I knew sounded foreign to their ears, so I wrote it on the black board. I repeated it several times and asked them to try saying it, which they did with varying degrees of success.

I told them I came from mid-America, the State of Minnesota. Unaccustomed as I was to extemporaneous speaking, I suddenly wondered how to explain to them about our cold weather and snow on the ground when they probably had nothing to relate it to. "When I left America, the place where I live, there was white snow," I began. "Do you know what snow is?"

They nodded. "The snow was this high," I leveled my hand thigh high. "When I left, it was 20 degrees below zero." I knew they couldn't even imagine it. I told them I was married, the mother of two children, my daughter was married and I was a grandmother to two little girls. I went on and told them I worked as a secretary at the University of Minnesota. I then turned the tables and asked them if they had any questions. Their hands flew up. One girl asked, "If I have a B.A. in Business, can I go to school in America and get an M.A. in English?"

I hadn't thought of that question. "You would have to get some basic credits in English in order to get a Masters degree," I answered. Then another young woman asked about credits and what they were. I tried to explain our method of choosing a class and earning a number of credits. When they earned enough credits, they could get their degree, I explained. How could I possibly let them know that I was no authority on college degrees, just a secretary trying to earn my own degree. They finally ran out of questions and I smiled, waved and headed for the door.

Out in the hall, a woman approached me and introduced herself. She was an Egyptian professor, Dr. Isitar, she explained in perfect English. She invited me to join herself and other teachers in the lunchroom for "something to eat and drink." I gladly accepted as she led me down the hall to a large well lit lunchroom, resembling our vendens in the University back home. We sat down at a table with four other professors. Enroute to the table we had stopped at the snack bar which featured several kinds of juices, coffee, tea and some sweets. I chose a can of apple juice which my hostess insisted on paying for. She was wonderfully gracious and friendly and she introduced me to the others as we sat down at the table. I was surprised when she said, "I earned my Doctor of Philosophy degree in the States, in Illinois". Dr. Isitar actually came from Cairo, Egypt, and she frankly reminisced nostalgically about attending college. "I love the States," she said, "and I miss that country".

Another lady professor offered the information that she had earned her Masters degree at the University of Kansas, while an Arabian native professor had studied in Switzerland. What a cosmopolitan group this was! All were congenial and we communicated beautifully. We spoke of many things, even able to laugh at taboo subjects. For example, I told them that some of my friends had asked me to bring back some oil. We all laughed together, even though it was a painful subject on both sides. The teachers break was over then, and I found Samia again. It was already 8:30 and Julie came out of her class, surprised to see that I was still there.

What followed then, was really unique to me. Classes were over for the evening, the students were standing near the gate waiting for their family chauffeurs to pick them up. The guard outside the gate called the family name as each chauffeur drove up. As each girl answered the call, her veil went down over her face as she ran out to get into the family limousine. I couldn't get over this veil business.

The young women wore no makeup, except kohl around their eyes, which were made up dramatically. Kohl is used much like we use mascara and eye pencil.

Julie and I rode in a chauffeur-driven University car with three other professors. We were a bit crowded, with two of us sitting in the front seat beside the driver and three in back. Two of the women had their veils on. All of them were wonderfully good natured, laughing often in friendly camaraderie. One lady said that this weather must feel very good to me, after coming from such a cold country. I agreed.

I asked a question about "Mother Eve's" grave. One of the learned women in the back seat of that beautiful Rolls Royce, rolling along the street of Jiddah in the brightly lit street of open booths, answered my question. "We truly believe Mother Eve is buried in Jiddah, because it says in our Koran (Bible) that Adam and Eve met at Mount Arafat after the 'fall'. That mountain is very close to Mecca; therefore, it is a reasonable belief," she said matter-of-factly.

When we arrived at the western compound where there were many walled-in houses, I said "Alle tu" to the driver and the ladies all laughed hysterically at me. It meant "drive on a little farther", but they got a kick out of my accent. One woman asked if I could possibly stay until Thursday because they would give an Arabian feed (a goat roast) for me . Reluctantly I declined, but wanted so much to find out what a goat roast was like. I dared not tell anyone that I now planned to visit Jerusalem on my way home. I apologized, "I'm sorry, but it's absolutely necessary for me to leave Monday morning." We said goodby and I sincerely thanked them all for the interesting experiences I had enjoyed. I especially thanked Julie, who reminded me that we would visit the Princess tomorrow.

What an adventure this evening had been. I don't think many outsiders had ever visited Abdul Aziz University, or would ever have the opportunity to visit a real Princess as I would the following evening.

Walking slowly toward the house, the realization that I would soon be leaving actually hit me. Everything I did now would be for the last time. Only one more day in Jiddah! It seemed as if soon I would awaken from this marvelous dream. I again noted how numerous the stars were and how close they seemed. I thought of the walled-in houses, the sandy streets, and all the new adventures I had experienced. I wished that it weren't coming to an end so soon.

Inside I found the evening was just beginning. Karl had

brought out his old slides and had the projector set up. His ensuing presentation unexpectedly jolted me back to reality. The slides he began to show were of our family back home a few years ago, but it served to remind me that my life was not this *Arabian Nights* thing. This had been a sojourn, a symbolic trip to Mecca of my own. The reality of my life was beckoning to me through the projected slides on the screen.

Some of the neighbors had come in; tall Clel from next door who ducked his head to get in the doorway, Jan Copeland, Chris and Roy Rogers. We watched slides that I never knew existed, of myself, my husband and kids, our dad and other relatives back home. Quite a change of pace from the earlier part of the evening. Still, the great differences that made Saudi Arabia really unique was because of the contrast to my life in America.

CHAPTER XVIII

PRINCESS JAWHARA/150 FREED SLAVES SERVE BANQUET/GOODBY JIDDAH

It was a most unlikely group gathered in the palace of Princess Jawhara on Sunday evening in Jiddah, Saudi Arabia and I was the most unlikely of all to be sitting in the receiving room of this influential royal Princess. This night, more than any other time since I arrived, I asked myself, "However did this happen to me, a nobody from small town America, waiting to meet the most influential woman in Arabia?" It meant that anything could happen to almost anyone, especially if you came from a country of citizens who were free to go wherever they wished -- or if you had relatives who invited you to visit them with a round trip ticket practically inserted in the invitation.

"Who is Princess Jawhara, Julie?" I asked on our way over there.

"You know that King Faisal is the absolute monarch of this country, don't you?" Julie asked patiently. I nodded. "This lady we are going to visit was his first wife when he was a Prince. She is also his first cousin. They loved each other, but Jawhara didn't give him a son in the first three years of their marriage, only a daughter. At the request of his father, King Abdul Aziz, the one who unified Saudi Arabia and helped win the country back from the Turks, Faisal divorced Jawhara. But, they say that Faisal and the Princess are very friendly and her influence and opinions are given high priority by the King."

We were driving through the palatial gates now and five guards waved us on, up the long curving driveway. "What do I say to her?" I asked Julie.

"Shake hands and say you're honored to meet her. She doesn't speak English, so I'll interpret for you. They say she understands more than she acknowledges -- much more English, I mean," Julie said, as she climbed out of the taxi first, careful not to trip over her long skirt. I followed. The drama was about to begin. The palace doorman opened the back door of the taxi for us. I was careful not to get any spots on my white "below-the-knees" dress. It was simple, but accented with matching red earrings and necklace.

Up the front steps and into a wide hallway we walked, seeing servants everywhere. In the foyer, they waved us on from the pillared hall straight ahead past small sitting rooms and into a large receiving room at least 60 feet long by 30 feet wide. A few of the women were clustered together on the couches closest to the door even though the walls were lined with frieze couches and chairs. It seemed a massive area. The six or seven women seemed minuscule at the one end.

Princess Jawhara's back was to us as we entered the room. She sat at the end of the room we entered. I was curious as to what she looked like. She was speaking in a loud, rather raspy voice in Arabic, deeply engrossed in conversation with the woman who sat to her left. Princess Jawhara presided from an overstuffed arm chair beside a telephone table alongside a black and white TV, at which she glanced occasionally even while she talked and gestured. Julie and I waited to be received. Julie informed me that the lady Jawhara conversed with was from Beirut. We were standing closer to the Princess now but she didn't acknowledge our presence while she was talking. However, Julie interpreted some interesting bits of their conversation.

"Jawhara is telling her that there wouldn't be so much crime in Lebanon if they would do like the Arabs in Saudi Arabia. If someone steals, cut off his hand, if he kills someone, he must die also. 'We have no crime in Arabia,' she is saying."

Now the Lebanese woman answered. I waited, fascinated as Jawhara leaned forward then, listening attentively. While Julie listened and interpreted the Arabic conversation, I appraised the Princess with the jet black hair and kohl drawn eyelids, wearing a long galibea that had a light background with large multi-colored polka dots stamped into it. Her matching polka dot shoes were unexpectedly modern. Long painted fingernails adorned hands dripping with gold and gemmed rings which I had found to be an interesting custom in the mideast. When Julie first whispered to me, I didn't really pay attention as I privately speculated upon the age of the Princess which could have been in the early sixties or again, much younger. I abstractedly considered the idea that the space between her two wide front teeth made her even more unattractive than necessary. If only she had been fitted with braces when she was a child. I amused myself by digressing that perhaps the Arabs didn't even know what braces were. That was an outgrowth of civilization which was obviously in "its infancy" here. But then I remembered how Arabians were masters of science, exploration and literature earlier than any other civilization. Now, I tuned into Julie. "She is telling Jawhara that the Lebanese believe in a different form of government than the Saudis. It's more of a democracy. They don't believe in such severe punishment," Julie said. At this moment Jawhara turned her fierce brown eyes our way, finally acknowledging our presence.

Julie introduced me to her in Arabic. The Princess extended her hand and we solemnly shook hands while looking directly into each other's eyes. Hers were dark and wary. She indicated with a gesture that we should seat ourselves on the couch beside two other ladies.

As Julie and I seated ourselves, the phone rang. Jawhara answered it herself and spoke loudly into it for about twenty minutes -- her voice low and guttural, speaking the Arabic so foreign to my ears.

Meanwhile Julie introduced me to the ladies who were sitting on the other side of the Princess, quietly waiting. She didn't know them all, but she was very self assured and introduced herself to those she didn't know, then introduced me. I had to admire Julie Akari -- she was really something.

I mentioned earlier it was a most unlikely group. First there was Ma'shael (Mashell), King Faisal's daughter, a large boned young lady who resembled her mother, the Princess. Julie whispered that she was in her thirties, had been married twice and had two children. Supposedly

Ma'shael didn't speak English, although she was taking English lessons. I met Mrs. Tiba Alattas, whose husband owns the largest hotel in Jiddah and Mrs. Su'ad Aljaffali, wife of the owner of the Power Company. Mrs. Aljaffali spoke English very well. She and Julie both translated for me during the course of the evening. As I sat beside her on the couch, servants were offering doll-sized cups of coffee and tea which Julie had warned me a visitor was required to accept, up to three cups at least. We took the small cups of coffee spiced with cardamon, and drank them quickly, then the servant came by with the tray and picked them up. Mrs. Aljaffali explained that all of the 150 servants who served the Princess had once been slaves. She had given them their freedom. (Saudi Arabia is still only a few years away from selling, buying and owning slaves from Africa). "She treats them like they are her own family," the light-haired Arab lady said. "They live in housing behind the palace, receive a small salary and are allowed to use the cars at times. She also sees to their education." There seemed to be servants standing around everywhere. Again we were offered coffee and mint tea, which we accepted.

I asked the Princess if she had ever been to America.

"No, not yet," she answered not looking at me. "I do not care to fly, and until now it has been too far."

"When I left Minnesota," I said, "the weather was 30 degrees below zero. Your weather is lovely. We had snow on the ground."

"You're lucky to come to Arabia where our weather is so nice," she answered and the ladies all laughed, probably not comprehending how cold 30 degrees below zero is. Their coldest weather is a balmy 65 degrees.

The large sitting room was well lit with nondescript colored walls, no pictures, but fabulously beautiful green velvet floor-length draperies. The rugs were marvelous oriental masterpieces. It seems as though everyone owns beautiful rugs in Arabia.

All during the evening the black and white TV at the side of the room was turned on. Naturally King Faisal was shown entering and departing his airplane, shaking hands with the other oil barons -- going into meetings, coming out of meetings, shaking hands with notables, etc. This is what most of the Arabian TV programming consists of. I asked Ma'shael if that was her father.

"My brother," she answered in faltering English.

"No, your father," Mrs. Aljaffali corrected her. "She takes English lessons," she said in an aside to me.

Princess Jawhara stood up suddenly. I thought she was about to retire and dismiss us all. We stood up, too.

"We must go," Julie said.

"Oh no," one lady said, "you must stay. We are just going to have a quick dinner." It was 10:30 p.m. I had heard they had late night dinners, but didn't expect to get in on one. The Princess led the six of us into the dining room. I couldn't believe my eyes at what I saw. The long banquet table literally overflowed with food. I had never seen such a variety of edibles in my life. The table was surrounded by black servants. Princess Jawhara washed her hands at a side table in a basin of water.

"Are we supposed to wash our hands?" I whispered to Mrs. Aljaffali.

She shook her head. "No, the Princess might eat with her fingers tonight, that's why she is washing hers."

After the Princess sat down at the head of the long table, we all sat down close together at one end. Each of our plates had one large spoon on it and I saw it was used for dipping into the various dishes and either tasting that particular food and/or heaping some of it on our own plates. There were at least 35 different varieties of meat dishes and vegetables all cooked in different ways. The whole smorgas - bord was laid out three times, so that everyone had access to every food without passing the dishes. Again I tried many kinds of food, all foreign to me, but very good. A few of them were: jireach (cracked wheat boiled for many hours with meat and spices), minced pie (potatoes, meat, spices and onions baked together), kapsa (rice cooked with meat and spices), toasted bread and plain flat Arabian bread with many kinds of homos to dunk it in (some made of mashed chickpeas, some of spinach mash).

Princess Jawhara actually didn't choose to eat with her fingers that night after all, but it is a common practice, Julie told me. Jawhara talked animatedly. I watched her in fascination through the whole meal with many gestures and expletives, I think. Then, unexpectedly she rose from the table, went to the side table and rinsed her mouth with water.

One lady remarked to me that she was sure I wished we (the U.S.A.) had some of their oil, referring to the TV on a stand which had been wheeled into the dining hall. King Faisal was still featured, meeting with his Arab cohorts, about the oil embargo which was very critical in February of this year.

I smiled and said, "Yes, it was very cold and we had many cars." The ladies all laughed. I said to the Princess that she should come to America sometime. It was then that she lashed out with, "We don't need America, but they need us. They know we are a power in the world." She was almost shouting now, although she wasn't even looking at me. She gazed off into the distance. Julie was standing beside me interpreting in a low voice. Jawhara was wiping her hands, now. "America has stabbed us in the back," she continued. "They give them (the Israeli Jews) everything -- everything they ask for and give us nothing! Once an Arab is hurt, he is hurt for good." She rose and headed for the sitting room again and motioned the rest of us to accompany her. We all rose and followed her obediently. I again sat on the couch at right angles to her chair, which was not a throne, but a high backed distinctive type straight-backed seat reeking of authority.

"But the Jews pay for what they get!" I answered, really not knowing if or what to say.

She appeared not to hear. "I know it's not the people of America, they have nothing to say about what the Government does. If they did, we wouldn't allow even one of you into our country. We'd send you all away just like that," she snapped her fingers.

Even if I could have gotten a word in at this point, I didn't want to argue with her about democracy or about the fact that we did have some say in the government. She raved on, "When Faisal visited the White House a few years ago to ask the President to stop giving the Jews all the money, guns, planes and everything they asked for, they just laughed at him. But now they know." She raised her index finger while her voice became louder and she spoke more rapidly. "Saudi Arabia is a power in the world. We do not need America -- but America needs us. If they take away our airplanes, we can ride camels. If they take away our food, we can grow our own." Her eyes were fiery. I was dumbfounded at this tirade and wished I knew what to say. One servant passed a bowl filled with large irregular chunks of resin. Everyone took a piece and chewed the mint spice like gum.

Jawhara also chewed lustily and then talked on, loudly, even harshly. "I don't understand it -- the Americans underestimated the Arabs by giving up the friendship of 100 million Arabs for two million Jews. I see no point to this!"

As if their eyes were synchronized, they all looked at the TV again as if frightened or embarrassed by this tirade. King Faisal was disembarking from his plane which had returned, reminding me that this moment could really become one of international consequence. I felt as though my answer might influence history. Even while I told myself this was a gross exaggeration, I was sure no American had been to visit Princess Jawhara, the most influential woman in Arabia for a long time. Partly because it is virtually impossible for an outsider to enter the country unless they have in-country sponsorship. My brother, Karl, had sponsored me, but there had been six months worth of red tape to go through to get into Arabia.

Consequently, this moment was very strained. "We sell them military equipment," I said, emphasizing the word "sell".

Tension stood in the room like a hostile person. No one spoke, hardly even breathed, as this fiery lady said, "America gives them everything! We get nothing! We were friends of America, and now we are not," she stated.

Faisal's father and Jawhara's mother had been brother

and sister, Mrs. Aljaffali whispered to me. "It is said that their marriage had been a love match long ago, but because Jawhara did not bear a royal son, only the one daughter, Faisal's father, King Saud, asked him to divorce her." I didn't tell her that Julie had already explained this to me, but it confirmed what Julie had said.

The maids now passed toothpicks to everyone. It is an Arab custom to pick food out of one's teeth after a meal. Jawhara became agitated again. "The Jews went in and threw the Palestinians out of their homes," she stated unequivocally. "How would you like it," she asked me casting her fiery dark eyes toward me," if your brother came and took your home away and then gave it to another brother? Would you like it?"

She waited for me to answer. While I tried to untie my eyes from the invisible chain that locked our eyes in a hypnotic trance, I finally shook my head. "I understand about the Palestinians now, since I've been here," I said. "I'll tell them about it in America when I return." Her analogy was startling. She said one brother takes your home away and gives it to another brother -- deep down the Arabs and Jews feel like they are half brothers under the flesh. The realization came as a staggering illumination. The Arabs are descended from Ishmael, the illegitimate son of Abraham, the patriarch of the Old Testament of the Bible; the Israelites are descended from Isaac, the legitimate son of Abraham and Sarah. Therefore, the Jewish people believe themselves to be the true possessors of the "promised land". Ishmael and Isaac were half brothers. Jawhara voiced this age-old truth in her remark. Mrs. Charlotte Al'Usaili, from Beirut, said, "There are signs posted all over America, which say 'Give a dollar to kill an Arab'."

"That's not true," I answered quickly. "I have never, never, even heard such a thing."

"When I was in Philadelphia several months ago and I went to a movie house, there was such a sign in the lobby," she said positively.

"I have never heard of such a thing," I repeated firmly.

"One quarter of a million Palestinians are homeless,"

Jawhara said as if there had been no interruption. "Because they were bombed and burned out of their houses -- or their houses were stolen from them. That is why we don't give you oil." I suddenly realized that at this moment, I symbolized America to her.

"What do you think of our Kissinger?" I asked changing the subject.

"He is all right," she said, but -- she put her palms up as if balancing the scales, "He is Jewish, too, you know."

On an impulse I took her hand, then, and looked her in the eyes and said to this Arabian Princess, who might now be the Queen if she had borne a son. "I only come here in friendship. I would like to be your friend," I smiled at her.

She looked at me for a moment out of dark angry eyes and then her anger appeared to fade. "I know it is not the American people," she said. "We are friends of the American people."

Hoping to find an agreeable subject, realizing with great clarity that the other ladies were listening to the Princess and myself exchanging slightly barbed remarks, I said, "I have never met a Princess before."

Mrs. Aljaffari asked, "Did you expect it to be like in *The Arabian Nights*?"

I laughed and nodded. They all laughed amiably. I really didn't know what I had expected, no one quite so accessible or ordinary as Princess Jawhara, I guess. I refrained from expressing this thought.

I then asked her to please visit us in America someday. She accepted. I told them all a bit about the University of Minnesota in Duluth where I am employed and I presented the Princess with two booklets put out in the Bureau of Business and Economic Research where I work. I also gave her one of my own historical research booklets which I had written. She thanked me while accepting them.

"You are very well known for your interest in the education of the women in Arabia," I said to her.

Princess Jawhara nodded apparently pleased at my interest. "I visited Dar-Al-Tarbia University last evening," I told her. "Mrs. Akari took me to school with her when she

127

taught her English class."

"What did you think of it?" Jawhara asked.

"I was impressed and thought it very beautiful."

"It is only three years old -- there are 500 girls enrolled," she said.

I thought it was fantastic progress for this to be happening in Arabia. Women have not been considered worth teaching until recent years. "Do you own Dar-Al-Tarbia?" I asked.

She nodded. "Who told you?"

"An American told me," I said. "It means 'House of Education'." She looked pleased and nodded.

It was after midnight and Julie suggested we go.

"Must you leave already?" the Princess asked as I shook hands with her.

"I leave for America at six in the morning," I answered. "Please come visit us sometime."

"When you come again perhaps you can spend more time with us," she said. Then she sent us back to the western compound in her chauffeur-driven American car. The multimillionaire's wives also rode with us. Of course they had to put their veils over their faces as they left the beautiful palace. Even the ultra and very powerful must don her veil when she goes out in public or speaks to a man in her own palace.

On the trip home, I wondered aloud how she felt about King Faisal. One of the ladies said they are on excellent terms and he consults her about many things. Faisal is married to 'Iffat', a lovely intelligent woman from Istanbul whose father was a Saudi and her mother Turkish. Their marriage has lasted over 30 years," Julie explained.

As I said goodby to the Saudi lades and Julie Akari at the compound, across the street from the luxurious Kandara Hotel owned by Mr. Alattas, whose wife was in the car, I felt as though some things about the old *Arabian Nights* stories were still true. I felt like Cinderella coming home from the ball. It was the crowning evening of many, in the month I spent in Jiddah.

My Arabian venture was now about to come to an abrupt

end. I left the car that night, went into the house directly to bed. Karl woke me at 4:30 a.m. before the sun had even opened one sleepy eye. I got up, dressed, finished packing my bags and without anyone awake to say goodby to, I took my leave. Karl drove me to the airport to board the jet plane which would take me to Athens. From there I would buy a ticket to Tel Aviv where new unknown adventures awaited me. I had no knowledge of where Jerusalem was, in relation to Tel Aviv where I would allegedly land sometime later today. Karl couldn't even whisper the name of Jerusalem in the airport that morning, so I kissed him goodbye, thanked him with all my heart and boarded the plane. Dawn was just breaking when the plane took off. What would tomorrow bring? No one in the whole world knew I was going to Israel except Karl and Margaret and they had no way of checking on me from where they were.

As the plane passed over the "Creek", I snapped a picture. Before dawn we had crossed the Red Sea. Then we flew over the legendary Sahara Desert which took hours even in the huge 747. Watching the desert below hour after hour became frightening because its vast emptiness spoke to me of crashing planes that were never found. I prayed for it to be left behind us. It seemed never-ending. The sky was cloudless and the sun blinding. I had to put my life in the hands of the Lord that morning when I left Jiddah with absolutely no idea of how or when I would get to Jerusalem. I only knew that I was almost out of money and that I had very little time to experience the places of Jesus in the promised land. This was Monday morning and on Thursday morning a plane left Athens for Paris, then not again until Saturday. I was due back at work next Monday morning, to a cold and unforgiving professor -- one week from today. I felt quite frightened and very much alone, but I knew I could trust the Lord to take care of me. I sat back in my seat wondering if I would really be in Jerusalem this very night. Where would I stay? The TWA plane was due out of Athens at noon. It was a TWA 747, so I needed to buy my ticket and report in two hours ahead of flight. I could only wait and see how it would all work out.

My sojourn to Biblical Arabia was already behind me and I knew I would relish every memory and fervently hoped that the pictures that I had sent out with people going to America would turn out. I closed my eyes to contemplate it all.

BOOK II

PASSAGE TO JERUSALEM

CONTENTS

JERUSALEM

PREFACE

The plane I was on, a B-747, was due in Tel-Aviv at 5:40 p.m. What to do or where to go once I was there? I didn't have a clue. We were sitting on the runway, looking at the greenery of Athens in February. I considered the Sahara desert we had flown over that morning. I wondered if most of Egypt was desert. Vast, vast eternal wasteland! Customs agents had made me lock my camera in my suitcase when in Athens. I didn't know why--I thought I had just left that kind of dictatorship in Arabia. We were up off the ground now--exhilarating! Just beyond the runway we were already out over the Aegean Sea. Hardly anyone on board spoke English, except the personnel who spoke it with thick accents. The scene out the window was wild with wind and waves swelling into housetop high breakers. In just seconds Athens was fading -- the sea was far below.

We landed in Israel. Getting off the plane, I first had to find somewhere to store my heavy baggage. I had brought many brass souvenirs from Arabia and couldn't possibly carry them with me. The girl at the information desk informed me that there were storage lockers across the street. The front door was close to the desk and opened onto a large circular street. When asked if I wanted to go to New Jerusalem or the Old City, I told her I didn't know the difference. She explained that the old City was the Arab Quarter, so I chose New Jerusalem because I was alone and everything was unknown to me. She called and reserved a room for me at Har Aviv on Beit Harkeren. Worst of all I then found there was only one bus going to Jerusalem from the airport and I missed it while finding storage for my luggage. I didn't even know that it was a 70 mile trip. I only knew that unless my fortunes started to improve, I was going to miss the experience of Jerusalem. Alone on the street I approached a patriarchal-looking Israeli with a long beard. "Sir," I asked in desperation, "how can I get to Jerusalem?" He shook his head indicating he couldn't speak English. English is the universal language, we hear, but on this side of the world I could hardly find anyone who spoke it.

Like an answer to a prayer, a pleasant looking dark-haired man, perhaps in his mid-thirties, standing at a bus stop a few feet away overheard me and noticed my evident dismay. In English with an accent which I couldn't discern, he said, "I am going to Jerusalem also. You have to buy a ticket in that little booth over there (a short distance away), take a bus to the end of the line here in Tel Aviv and then transfer. Watch me. I also missed the bus from the airport." What else could I do, but follow his advice?

I let the girl in the ticket booth choose the coins I had exchanged in the airport. I had only changed $30 worth of Travelers Checks, never dreaming that it would hardly even get me to Jerusalem, but my money was running very low-- all I had was about $90. Our dollar was currently worth about 4.50 pounds. Now the bus, overflowing with people, had stopped to pick us up. I had to stand on the dilapidated, lurching vehicle. My long dress (gallibea) seemed a bit out of place, but I didn't know what the accepted attire was in Israel. When it was sewn in Jiddah, the long green and white thobe fit in well with their explicit laws and customs. Furtively glancing at the people around me, I noticed they dressed more like we do in America, rather than like the veil-draped Arabian women. The men wore pants instead of long thobes such as mine. I had two heavy sling bags plus my purse to carry and the ride was really bumpy. Half an hour like this seemed like an eternity.

Finally we came to the end of the bus line. Following the dark haired man, I found we were still in Tel-Aviv and had at least another hour's ride to Jerusalem. He and I stood at the bus stop--it was already dark. He said he was from Montreal which explained the now obvious French accent.

An interminable time elapsed and the others at the stop stood in stoic silence, apparently weary. We finally found out through a series of signs and gestures that we could get a taxi a block away to go to Jerusalem. We walked down the street as the sun slipped down over the horizon. We agreed to split the cost and hire a taxi, little knowing that it was still a long way to Jerusalem. A surly Arab lounged against a cab that looked like it should have been junked. The driver, let us know it would cost 55 pounds or 20 dollars to drive us there. We were both very tired and decided to hire him. Darkness had already set in when we stepped into the cab.

My companion was a sturdy, handsome man with serene blue eyes. His blue sailor top and maroon pants fit well on his 5'8" frame. We didn't speak at first as the noisy car bumped along the road. "Are you a priest?" I asked him. He was surprised. "Why do you ask?"

"I don't know", I answered.

"You guessed right. I'm on my way back to my mission in Central Africa," he explained. "I have been stationed in Africa for 12 years. I belong to the White Missionary Fathers, but I've been sick and was sent home to Montreal with my family for a year's recuperation.

"What sickness did you have?" I asked into the blackness.

"I suffered from hepatitis for three years. I couldn't rest because there was so much to do and I couldn't recover," he said almost apologetically. "Finally they sent me home to Canada to my family to recuperate."

When we finally arrived in New Jerusalem, the driver asked a passerby on the dark lonely street where Har Aviv was. My companion's name was Gaeton Poulin. His French accent was so thick that the driver couldn't understand him at all. So even though he was heading for St. Anne's in the old city of Jerusalem, he got out of the cab with me and we walked downstairs to a basement lunchroom. It was dreary with dim lights and had four square tables in it. Gaeton looked around for a phone. There was a short thin man down there who spoke only

133

German and Hebrew. Frustrated with trying to communicate with us, he finally got on the phone and talked to someone who we assumed might speak English. We managed to get a cup of coffee through gestures to the man. Gaeton found an English telephone book and eventually figured out how to call the number at St. Anne's, but no one answered the phone. He called another cab which took a long time to come. Then he took off into the night hopefully headed for St. Anne's in the so-called Arab quarter. He promised to call me at this number if and when he arrived to let me know if there was a mass in the morning. I hadn't been to church in almost a month since only Moslems are allowed to worship God in Arabia.

Now I was alone in the dreary place with the bespectacled little man. He beckoned me to follow him across the street and into a house behind a house. The darkness was like black ink. He rang the bell on the barred gate. A answering buzz from inside opened the gate. A middle-aged woman who looked hard and old for her years met us and, in English, introduced herself as Mrs. Buechler. She looked hard and old for her years. "Did he tell you we have only a double room and not a single?" she asked abruptly. I shook my head. "It will cost more," she stated. "I have no more singles tonight."

"How much in American dollars?" I asked.

She answered, $8.50 a night."

I had no recourse but to take it, although I wondered if I'd be able to pay my way out of there. Karl had given me the $200 for plane fare and out of the meager $300 I had brought with me, I had less than $100 and I had halfway around the world to go yet.

My new landlady, looking severe, led me upstairs to a room which was cold when she opened the door. The temperature both inside and out must have been in the low forties. There were two single beds in the medium size room. The walls were painted a sickly light green. There were no pictures on the walls and the windows were not glass, but were covered with heavy venetian blinds. I shivered as she turned on the radiators. After she closed the door behind herself, I ran into the bathroom and turned on some steamy hot water. The bathtub was a wonder! I couldn't wait to get in. It was porcelain with half of it five inches higher than the other half. I sat in the wonderful hot water on one level and rested by legs on the other. In the warmth, I almost forgot about the worry of the next day. "Why don't we have tubs like this back home", I wondered? I was hardly finished soaking when I was startled by a knock on the door. You have a telephone call downstairs, a young female voice informed me.i I threw on my robe and ran down the stairs to answer. It was Gaeton sounding far away who said he had arrived at St. Anne's and he would celebrate mass there at 8:30 in the morning. He told me in a barely audible voice that it was a 30 minute ride to the Old City, but I should direct the cab driver to take me to St. Stephen's Gate and he, Gaeton, would be there to meet me. I thanked him and assured him I would be there at 8:30. I was grateful and elated. The answer to my prayers, I thought. I had only two precious days. Mrs. Buechler turned her back as I thanked her. She was neither friendly nor helpful.

Then I slept! It was so good to sleep. Only that morning at 5:30 I had still been in Jiddah on the Red Sea, which, although it was two countries away, wasn't really so far. Only Karl and Margaret knew where I was and they were unable to communicate with me from that Arab country.

CHAPTER I

JERUSALEM

When I woke at 7 a.m. without the benefit of an alarm clock, I jumped up quickly, looking at the iron barred window-doors hardly able to believe that I was in Jerusalem. Jerusalem! Center of the world! However, I was in the new City of Jerusalem and still half an hour's ride from the old walled city. I walked rapidly across the street from the rooming house, eagerly anticipating the once in a lifetime day I was about to live. I hurried downstairs to a basement lunchroom to relish a cup of hot cocoa, a sweet roll and cheese, the continental breakfast which was included in the cost of the plain room I had rented. The little man who spoke only German and Hebrew understood me well enough to call a cab. I rode in front with the Arab driver and even managed to carry on a bit of conversation as we drove across the busy modern city of New Jerusalem. His English was extremely limited and I couldn't speak his native tongue at all. Soon we wound up the road to the outside of the walls of the beloved city. My breath caught in my throat.

Suddenly he stopped at the gate called the Lion's Gate (a lion's head is carved into the wall above it), also called St. Stephen's Gate, one of eight gateways into the walled city). The fare was seven pounds or about $1.75. Gaeton Poulin was standing inside the gate right in front of St. Anne's waiting for me. I was so happy to see a familiar face.

Father Gaeton Poulin led me through the main basilica whose high rotunda echoed with hammers and drills in the early morning sunshine. I later found that restoration is constantly carried on at almost every shrine in the Holy City. Gaeton led the way downstairs to the Chapel of the Annunciation where he said the Mass of the Annunciation. I knelt on the altar steps and responded to the priest as he

136

said the Mass. It was marvelous! Again I couldn't believe this was actually happening to me!

Here I was, this cool sunny morning in February of 1974 hearing mass in St. Anne's Church. In Jerusalem this chapel is sometimes presumed to be the site of the Annunciation. Father was now asking me to read aloud the epistle for the day. The hammers were pounding so loudly in the echoing chambers upstairs that at times I couldn't even hear him. I was the only participant at this mass and when I received the Lord in Communion, my heart overflowed with gratitude and thanksgiving.

Then mass was over. Right down the ancient hall was another chapel at the place where Mary was suppose to have been born. A statue of a baby girl reposed there. There are various beliefs about this, but who is to know? Joachim, her father, spent much time in Jerusalem in the Temple.

We went upstairs again now, through the Church of St. Anne and around to the back where ancient pilings and an old rock stairway were all that remained of the pool of Bethesda. The remains are just crumbling ruins, but this was the site where Jesus cured the lame man who had lain for 38 years in abject despair. I followed Fr. Gaeton down the railingless steps and found them very precarious. There was no one else around that early morning except the workmen in the Church. Climbing back up seemed just as dangerous as going down, but it certainly made everything seem authentic. No tourist commercialism here.

Then Fr. Poulin said that unfortunately, (for him), none of the priests at St. Anne's were free to be with him today, so he would also be alone and allowed that we might as well walk the City together. I was delighted because I was playing every minute by ear, really praying the Holy Spirit would arrange things for me. We found a little fold-up map at a small outdoor tourist store and were surprised to see that we were actually standing at the beginning of the Via Dolorosa or Way of the Cross, right outside of St. Anne's Church. The front door opened unto the cobblestone walkway. A short distance up the walk a tall cross, that

137

pilgrims carried up the Via Dolorosa every Friday, was propped against a wall. We learned t. But this was Monday. I tried pulling it away from the wall, but it was so heavy that I didn't have the strength to budge the monstrous piece of wood which was supposedly the same approximate size and weight of Jesus' cross.

We continued to walk up the narrow marketplace street where merchants hawked their wares to tourists like ourselves. The street was covered by overhead archways and flowed with many kinds of people: black ladies carrying baskets on their heads, Arab men with their traditional headscarves wrapped around their heads, old Jewish men, Yemenis men, a few Moslem ladies with little veils over their faces (here only up to their eyes, not like over their heads as in Arabia). Such a motley conglomeration of people that it was easy to imagine how Jesus and His disciples walked all over the City, most often unnoticed. Also, many Arab men and boys blocked our way begging to be our guides to individual shrines. I found out later that most of these men were Palestinian Arabs who had been bombed out or thrown out of their homes by the Jews coming into the country in need of more room. They weren't able to get other jobs because they were treated like people without a country.

We had begun to pass the Stations of the Cross--these were the places where the depicted scenes actually happened. We passed with awed reverence the almost inconspicuous plaques where Jesus met His dear Mother, the spot where Veronica wiped His bloodstained face and where He fell. Many of these sites had convents or shrines which one entered right off the street. You didn't realize they were there unless you looked behind the great doors which seemed to be part of the enclosed wall of the marketplace. It was much like the suk (sook) in Arabia where I had just spent a month. Finally the last stations brought us into the courtyard of the Church of the Holy Sepulchre. We came on it through what we would call an alleyway. We said "no" to the Moslem guides who made a living telling the Christians that this was actually Calvary

MAP OF JERUSALEM

THE LION'S GATE I.E. ST. STEPHEN'S GATE,
ENTRANCE TO ST. ANNE'S CHURCH

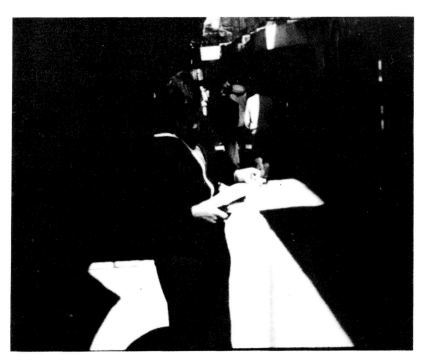

FATHER POULIN STUDYING MAP OF JERUSALEM

AN OVERVIEW OF THE DOME OF THE ROCK I.E. MOSQUE OF OMAR

AN INSIDE VIEW OF THE CHURCH OF THE HOLY SEPULCHRE,
CHRISTIANS MOST SACRED SHRINE

A PIECE OF THE ROCK OF JESUS' TOMB LIES BENEATH THE ALTER OF THE
COPTIC CHAPEL ADJOINING THE EDICULE OF THE CHURCH OF
THE HOLY SEPULCHRE

VIEW OF JERUSALEM FROM GETHSEMANE, NEAR THE DUNG GATE

GAETON POULIN ON ROOFTOP OF HOUSE, ATTEMPTING TO ASSESS
THE LAY OF THE LAND-GETHSEMANE IN BACKGROUND

and, adjacent to it, the site of Christ's tomb inside this ancient basilica. There was scaffolding in the portico of this most holy shrine and we walked under the ladders and scaffolding to enter the church. Workmen were pounding, rebuilding and restoring.

Inside we climbed steep, old and decaying cement stairs to a chapel built on the hill known to be Calvary. Outside the chapel an old Greek Orthodox priest gave us a vial of holy oil in return for an offering. A group of noisy tourists had followed us up the stairs so Father and I sat outside the chapel and listened to their guide's explanation of Calvary. We sat and meditated and prayed, both enveloped in our own deep thoughts even though the noise and confusion from the people and the restoration made it hard to concentrate. But I knew I would forever cherish that moment as I looked at the variety of mosaics on the floors (all mosaic tile), and the archways that led into the chapel, with their walls totally covered with art intermixed with a variety of frescoes of Jesus the Christ. Over the gleaming gold altar was a huge painting depicting Jesus being nailed to the cross while his Blessed Mother looked on. Vigil lamps made of gold and silver hung everywhere throughout the shrine. Vigil candles burned all the time. Every wall and ceiling was different, perhaps left by different conquering peoples who all put their individual kind of imprint on this one and only Calvary. Reluctantly Father Poulin and I pulled ourselves away each one knowing we had much to see yet in a very limited time span. We went down the steep stone stairs to the other side of the Church where the grave was marked by a huge marble plaque, the size and shape of a coffin. This area was all blocked in with marble and gold. The great scene of the Resurrection was emblazoned in gold as well as the tabernacle, all the hanging altar lamps and many candlesticks. Fresh flowers adorned the shrine. I had never realized how geographically close the Crucifixion and the burial were to each other. The tomb had to be very close in order to bury the body before the sabbath began on that infamous day when the Passover was upon the people of Jerusalem.

"This was the place that made what Jesus said totally credible," Gaeton said. "Without this burial/ resurrection, we could never have had the sure knowledge that our faith is really from God--that Jesus was truly His son." We meditated the best we could in the great echoing basilica, then passed on outside through the scaffolding, ladders and tourists. There we looked at our little folding maps. Where to now?

We found the Upper Room where the revered Last Supper may have taken place on the map, then tried to figure out which direction David's Citadel was and were amazed to find it was all incorporated in the same complex. But we had lost our sense of direction in the closed streets. The outside stairways leading to the rooftops of the surrounding houses might be the only way to get our bearings. We climbed one staircase and ducked through flapping clothes drying on the lines. From here, on this typically flat roof, we could see everything in all directions. On one side was the wide Mount of Gethsemane. In a moment of perception, I realized that old Jerusalem is in a flat valley and the Dome of the Mosque is on the same side as Gethsemane. We could see from the map that David's burial place was in the opposite direction. We could even see it from that rooftop. We walked down the rickety steps at the side of the flat-roofed house and began to hike toward David's tomb.

"It seems funny not to see any cars inside this wall," I said to Gaeton. As we walked, I noted how many different races of people we passed. "We are probably the most out-of-place people around," I said, "but no one seems to notice. I was amazed at the goats and sheep who wandered the street.

We walked up the dusty road to the huge complex which is built into or is an integral part of the wall. "This is David's Citadel," Gaeton said in awe. Inside the gate, the crumbled walls and ruins spoke of recorded and unrecorded kinds of civilizations. We later read that some different nationalities represented included: Hasmonean, Herodian, European Crusaders and others. This was believed to have been a part of the City of David so many thousands of years ago, old almost beyond comprehension. The Synagogue and sarcophagus (burial place) of King David is here. In an adjoining building, a memorial chamber is dedicated to the 6 million Jews of the Nazi Holocaust. We climbed up a narrow flight of railingless brick stairs to the Coenaculum (the Upper Room) where Jesus and the Apostles purportedly ate the Last Supper, the first Eucharistic banquet.

It was mid afternoon, (the sun was already waning a bit), a magnificent spring day this Monday, February 20. I felt warm even with my light lavender spring coat on.

As we walked across the wide wall from the stairs to the "Upper Room". We saw an empty room with two fireplaces and an old, cracked floor. The sun slanted through the one window over the door, ethereally spotlighting one bright sunbeam on the floor. There were pillars in the center of the room.

"It's empty," I said. Fr. Gaeton nodded. We each sat by a different fireplace and did our own meditating. Not another person was around this quiet deserted place. Compared to the Church of the Holy Sepulchre the silence was uncanny.

I tried to visualize those historic hours when Jesus instituted the Holy Eucharist, His own body and blood. Tradition also says that this was the room where Mary, the Apostles and other friends of Jesus came after the crucifixionto hide and wait. Christ appeared to them here after the Resurrection and the Holy Spirit came upon them. It really hasn't changed so very much, I thought. Although so many different peoples had conquered and changed the landscape of Jerusalem, still the atmosphere remained old and unhurried and integrated with many kinds of people--as it had always been.

Time was of the essence now, and there was so much more to see. We had no route to follow and people only gave us information if we paid them for it, so we were on our own with our little maps, which we tried to follow.

Before we left Mount Zion, we walked past the Church of the Dormition. It was marked on our maps with no

141

explanation, but we stopped there and went inside the enclosure where we found an old priest walking in a beautiful garden outside the church, reading his prayer book. He looked up as we came in, seeming annoyed that we disrupted his reverie, dug his cane into the ground and said brusquely, "Yes?"

I asked him what shrine this was explaining who we were and that we were trying to find our own way around Jerusalem. He told us he was Father Tomacek, an American Franciscan, who lived here at the shrine where Mary was believed to have "slept away" or died before her body was placed in the tomb from where she was assumed into Heaven.

"That's amazing," I said. "I've never heard of the place where Mary died before." He kind of smiled at that as he took out his keys to open the door of the church and lead us down into the cellar (tomb) where a statue of Mary lay, as if reposing.

I could hardly take it all in. So much had apparently happened inside the walls of the Old City, an enclosure you could walk in one day. I had never realized it.

We went upstairs into the beautiful, very high domed cathedral. Father Tomacek, who was now very friendly to Father Gaeton and myself, told us there was a Benedictine school here and that the shrine was cared for by the Franciscans. Father even showed us his own private quarters, a comfortable suite of rooms surrounded by a garden patio. He said there were three other Franciscans who lived there, too. We thanked him then and moved on.

Down the narrow gravelly path we walked, until we came to another church, where a busload of pilgrims waited. They were Dutch people, apparently waiting for the sisters to open up the Church. The siesta time prevails in the afternoon and that's why it was so quiet. We found the Shrine was called St. Peter in Gallicante, "the place where Peter cried". We waited for about 20 minutes or more, but the sister didn't appear, so we decided we must go on.

The path or narrow little road we were on was outside the city wall in this particular place and we were heading toward

A LOOK DOWN THE VIA DOLOROSA

CITADEL OF KING DAVID

DORMITION ABBEY WHERE
MARY IS BELIEVED TO HAVE
BEEN ASSUMED INTO
HEAVEN AFTER HER DEATH

DOWN IN CRYPT WHERE
MARY IS BELIEVED TO
HAVE BEEN ASSUMED
INTO HEAVEN AFTER
HER DEATH

Gethsemane. We were so terribly hungry, but didn't know where to get any food. We saw a small grocery-type store and managed to get some cookies and Coca Cola to ease our starving stomachs. We didn't even see a place where we could eat these packaged cookies until we finally crossed a little bridge over a dried up stream (wadi) and we sat on the cement wall. We did not realize until later that this little bridge overlooked the ancient City of David which is probably why his palace was on Mount Sion (what I would have called a hill). It felt great to sit down on the stone wall and eat cookies and drink Coca Cola in the sun. We had already walked far since that morning.

Two dark skinned ladies, heads covered by shawls, came walking by with two little children who hung back from their mothers and looked hungrily at our cookies. Father offered them some and I snapped a picture of them taking cookies while the two ladies with the white head coverings watched and smiled. A charming picture.

As we walked along the dusty path, we came upon a small domed chapel where two Moslems were bent over praying. An Arab asked us if we wanted to hire him to tell us about the tomb of Mary or this place of her Assumption. We were both very low on funds and told him so, but we did go inside. On either side of the staircase were supposedly the tombs of Sts. Anne and Joachim. By now it was late afternoon and the only person in the tomb was the custodian who was sweeping the floor. We looked around and saw only crumbling walls and many silver and gold vigil lights hanging from the ceiling. The walls were of brick and looked as though they had somehow been swept by fire at some ancient time. Old Jacobi, the friendly little olive skinned man, told us his name and told us this was the place where Mary's body had been buried and from where she was assumed into Heaven. I looked at it with interest, but it was just a cement slab. Itwas gouged, as though people had scratched at it to take home a few pieces of the rock.

Jacobi leaned on his broom and told us he was American Catholic and had been the sacristan of Mary's tomb for many years. He spoke English fluently (he could speak circles around Gaeton who hadn't spoken English in the whole year he had been home in Montreal). Jacobi showed us an ancient passageway where the early Christians had crept into the tomb to pray at this sacred spot.

"The Church was once built above ground," he explained as the sun slanted down the 50 or more stairs and spotlighted one wall. "But, it was destroyed and rebuilt many times, until finally they just built this little shrine down where the actual tomb is." He started sweeping again. He was short, very nice looking, soft-spoken and sincere. I observed the tomb more closely, and I had to look straight up see to the vaultied ceilings. I now saw that all the hangings were not necessarily vigil lights, some of them were actually elaborate candelabra, maybe even crystal. There were hundreds of hanging lights in the tomb. The tomb was carved right out of the rock, Jacobi told us. On some parts of the brick-like floor, there were lovely Persian rugs. The whole place had a golden glow about it.

As we walked around, Jacobi offered some interesting information pointing to the gouged-out rock that the tourists had vandalized so they could take home a relic. "That is not of the real slab where Mary's body was," he said confidentially. Somehow, I believed him because he had nothing to gain by being nice to two moneyless tourists. "I actually have some of the original."

"You do?" I asked incredulously.

He nodded. "It's in a little box back in my closet--a few pieces that I have in my possession that are very special."

We talked with him some more. I told him how I came from Minnesota, one of the United States, and a little bit about my family, how I had two children and worked at the University. Fr. Gaeton told him he was a White Father on his way back to his mission in Central Africa. No one disturbed our short little get-acquainted talk. I think tourists were not coming in this February day, because Golan Heights was the theatre of war now and it wasn't far from Jerusalem. We had heard occasional firing as we walked. It did sound to the world like it was dangerous to be in Jerusalem right now because there actually was a war going on.

We were about to go back up the wide stairs, in fact I had never seen such a wide stairway. There were 100 easy stairs to climb. Then I dared to ask Jacobi, "Would you consider giving us a teeny, small piece of the relic of the slab? I would take mine back to America and Father would take his back to Africa with him." I didn't really think he'd part with it, but surprisingly he turned and went directly to a little closet, hidden in the decor. There were about 10 rounded wooden panels, like half-walls, and the second one opened to his little closet. He brought out a small box and took out three small white pieces of stone for each of us. "You can crush this and make the slivers into a hundred relics," he said. We shook his hand and thanked him, feeling so good that someone in Jerusalem ha done us a true unusual kindness just out of goodness of his heart. We couldn't even tip him or give him an offering. Gaeton was as happy as I was about it. This quiet priest of about 40 years was very nice to be with in Jerusalem. He was a very serious and holy person.

CHAPTER II

GETHSEMANE

We hurried up the many stairs and crossed the main highway which goes by the west wall of Jerusalem. We passed the golden gate which was sealed up and had been for many centuries, up to the road to Gethsemane. The Mounts were to me like walking up the hills of Duluth and we aren't in the mountains at all in Minnesota. But our eyes were fixed on the part of the hillside where the rock of the agony reposed. We passed the Six Day Memorial of the Jewish people and hurried our steps. This monument was in memory of the 1967 war with Syria when many Israeli soldiers were killed. There were different boys and men who occasionally stopped us hawking souvenirs or offering to give us a tour, but we told them we had no money. We could see they really couldn't comprehend how two people from the North American Continent could be way over there without any money, nor did they probably believe it, but it was certainly true and my small supply was dwindling even now. I had halfway around the world to travel and was really almost broke--oh well, the Lord would provide. I had to leave it to Him. After all He got me here. What was sad was that there was a little Arab boy with the most beautiful soft brown eyes I had ever seen who wanted to sell me a photograph of Jerusalem. He had followed us from Mary's tomb up the hill to Gethsemane. It was a long rolled up picture that he was sure I would buy from him and I just couldn't. At the very end, he finally gave it to me for about 50 cents, which was a steal, and I was grateful to get it, even though that poor little fellow was so disappointed with the small amount of money.

There were several tourist buses that passed us on this winding road because cars can travel outside the walls, even though the road is so narrow that it is barely wide enough for a regular size bus or car. As we looked back, we

146

didn't realize that the wide gully we had crossed before crossing the highway was the famous Kiddron Valley where St. Paul often stayed when he came to Jerusalem. Also, Jesus and the Apostles walked through that dusty valley every time they came to the garden hillside. And probably everyone in the Bible knew and had come through it.

As we climbed higher and higher up this Gethsemane hill, we looked back and realized one could see the whole of Jerusalem from almost any part of it. It well spanned the width of the wall of the City, a marvelous breathtaking view. We were now at the Church of all Nations. It had twelve domes, each one donated by a different nation of the world. Inside this lovely Church the altar is built around the rock of the agony. It is enclosed by iron grillwork, just as outside the church the ancient olive trees which are more than 2,000 years old are enclosed by iron grillwork. They are gnarled stumps that saw the agony of the God-man. "Oh, rock of ages and trees from ancient times, what tales you could tell us if you had the ability to speak our language--or if we could but speak yours", I thought poetically. These ancient living monuments are the only things that were really here way back then. All else, including the walls of Jerusalem have been built and rebuilt, their enclosures varied over the long centuries since Jesus came to walk upon His created earth.

While we stood there on Gethsemane as the sun was about to dovetail, a well dressed Arab approached us. He began talking to us about Gethsemane. Right away we told him we had no money to pay for information, but he continued to talk to us in a very friendly manner. The well dressed, dapper white shirt and tie man told us he was a Palestinian who made his living guiding tourists. He told us all about the whole Mount of Gethsemane. He pointed out how the narrow walled-in road wound up and up toward the top of the Mount. Along the way there were several chapels and churches, Faride (Fa reed) pointed out. We now realized that we had seen all we could for today. The sun had disappeared, the air was cool now and we still had to walk back from the Place of the Agony and find our way into the old City--and I had to get back to my lodgings in New Jerusalem, alone. But, thank God for Fr. Gaeton's companionship this day, I thought. Before we started down the road I asked Faride if he knew of Father Godfrey, an American priest whom a Lady in Duluth had told me to be sure to find if, and when I got to Jerusalem.

"Of course," said Faride. Father Godfrey lives right here at the Church of All Nations. I'll inquire if he is in." This really surprised me because I never would have believed that I would be at his front door when I asked about him. Faride knocked at the door of the Rectory, but the housekeeper said that Father was out with some visitors. He apparently is the "Guide of Jerusalem". We left word that Father Poulin and I wished to see him and that we could return in the morning. At this moment, I breathed a prayer to the Holy Spirit about tomorrow because Father Poulin was supposed to go somewhere else with the priests from St. Anne's and I didn't really feel comfortable being alone in this strange land. But I wouldn't worry about it, I knew it would somehow be taken care of. In the old City of Jerusalem there was such a variety of peoples, Arab men who still wore the Moslem headdress, old Jewish men who looked to be as old as the City itself, veiled lades, young Arab men and boys who wandered about looking to be guides to tourists and Africans with jugs on their heads. All were foreign to me, few spoke English.

Meanwhile, Fr. Gaeton asked Faride where we could get some supper. He must have been as starved as I was--only cookies, hot chocolate and soda all day. I was achingly tired and getting chilled now. Faride walked down the hill of Gethsemane with us. We walked back across the dried-up river bed of the Kiddron Valley. To the right of the Golden Gate we took the walkway outside the wall and soon came to a small business district. There we saw a restaurant for about the first time that day. Faride was kind enough to go in with us and help us order a kind of sandwich called Schwamme or some such word--a Middle East kind of sandwich. It had some meat on the flat, tasteless (to me) Arabian bread wrapped around it. It was fairly good, but more important, it was filling.

Over supper, Faride told us about himself. He was a Palestinian who lived in nearby Bethany (at this time we didn't realize this was the village where Jesus stayed when He came to Jerusalem with Lazarus). He told us in his free and easy talkative way that he had a wife, five children and owned two houses.

"When my father died he left his house to me," Faride said. He tilted his debonaire hat. I could see he loved to put on a cosmopolitan air. He spoke in Hebrew to the owner of the eatery and told us he had kept the man from overcharging us. At least that's what he said--we couldn't know how truthful Faride Zahoor actually was, but at least he had befriended us when we needed a friend.

CHAPTER III

A NIGHT IN NEW JERUSALEM

Faride Zahoor told us he had a cab driver friend who would drive to Bethlehem for 20 pounds if either or both of us wanted to go there the next day. My morning cab driver had quoted me 30 pounds. Faride said he would bring his taxi driver friend up the Mount of Olives to the Chapel of the Ascension the next day and meet us at the Chapel if we decided to go. Because Gaeton didn't know if he would be busy elsewhere tomorrow or not, we said we'd try to make it.

We left the restaurant, each of us going our separate ways. I had to go outside the great gate called the Dung Gate to hail a cab to take me back to my quarters in New Jerusalem, the City where the Knesset and other government buildings were located. I felt quite alone and a little fearful now, but at least I had the assurance that Father Poulin would be saying Mass at 8:25 a.m., and I said hopefully I'd be at St. Anne's at that time.

The cab driver spoke little English and we rode the long dark way back to Har Aviv in literal silence. I got out of the cab and walked down the street hoping to find a drug store, but had no luck. The streets were darker than the deepest countryside, so I returned to my room and took a most welcome hot bath--brr, I shivered in the coldness of the room. It had begun to warm up as I turned on the heat when I opened the door to the bleak room. I had gotten very chilled in the February cold of Israel. I soaked gratefully in that beautiful hot water. I loved the bathtub. It really warmed me up. I noticed from here the high barred bathroom window beside which hung a large key. When getting out of the tub, I climbed up to get it and looked around to see what that key might fit. In the bedroom I could see an iron enclosure outside the sliding window/door. Feeling like an explorer, I slid that door open and found myself outside on a small enclosed porch-like place behind the great iron gate. There was a large keyhole which the key fit into. I opened it and went out into the blackness of the night. My own private entrance! The houses were all built one upon the other, most of them looked like apartments or rental rooms. I walked gingerly staying close to the side of the house and soon came to the front entrance, but it seemed like a puzzle in the dark. A deadly silence reigned even though it was only about 10:30 p.m. Nothing moved anywhere, except me. I retraced my steps, thinking this was exciting. I laughed silently to myself at this thought and found my way back to the iron gate, let myself in and locked the gate behind me. I then went out the inside door to find Mrs. Buechler, the landlady, to ask if she would wake me at 7 a.m. She agreed, but was not friendly to me. She was a hard looking Jewish lady who recoiled from me when she heard my German name. Later, I found she had spent seven years in a Nazi concentration camp--no wonder my very name sent her into a shell. I returned to my room and wrote in my diary for several hours, fully aware that the events of tomorrow would make me forget the sequence of events from today. After midnight, I finally fell into bed, asleep almost immediately, a busy, but well spent day over.

Strangely enough I had fitful dreams about Mrs. Buechler's daughter whom I had seen earlier. She had been in her mother's quarters with a small child when I had been there to use the phone. She was a young married woman who told me her husband was in the Israeli army and was fighting at Golan Heights from where I had heard the guns when in old Jerusalem that very day. She was pretty and much friendlier than her mother. She had been watching a small black and white TV. I asked her how I could get back to Tel Aviv to take the early morning plane to Athens. She explained that I must call and reserve a seat in a charute taxi. "There are seven seats in each taxi and they pick you up out in front of the house on the corner," she told me. She called the number for me and I talked to the dispatcher, who spoke very bad English. He told me he would have the taxi come by on Thursday morning at 4:45 a.m., so I could make the 8 a.m. 747 plane to Athens. I reserved a seat even though I didn't know how I would make that early morning connection. This night I dreamed I missed the taxi--a real nightmare when I had no money. The landlady's daughter spoke English as though it were her first language. I think she was watching an old American movie with Hebrew subtitles. When I slept, the night was over like the flick of an eyelash.

CHAPTER IV

SECOND DAY

I overslept. Mrs. Buechler didn't wake me up, so it was already 8:30 when I woke with a start. I dressed quickly, hailed a cab outside and somehow made the driver understand that I wanted to go to St. Ann's. It took about 30 minutes. Finally the cab wound up the hill to the great St. Stephen's gate. Father Gaeton was waiting for me--he hadn't celebrated the mass yet. I was grateful--he knew I'd be coming, he said in his serious way. The cab cost between 7 and 10 pounds, or $1.75 to $2.25. It differed each time I rode in one.

Again I was the only participant at the Chapel of the Annunciation and Father celebrated the Mass of St. Clare, the associate of St. Francis of Assisi and founder of the Poor Clares. I felt good about him choosing that saint. It was much like the day before, the noise of the workmen, sometimes almost deafened me in that huge basilica, even though we were downstairs in the same little Chapel of the Annunciation.

After Mass, another quick walk to the Pool of Bethesda and then we set off in the cool, but sunny morning for Gethsemane to see Father Godfrey. Because we were later than we had promised, he had already left with a morning tour group, but he did leave word that he'd return at 3:30. We ran into Faride again outside near the garden of the Church of all Nations where we looked in awe at the great knotted, gnarled old olive tree whose girth may have taken the arm span of six or seven men. We confirmed our noon taxi appointment to Bethlehem. Gaeton had somehow been left out of the other Priest's plans for today, too, except at 3:30 he was supposed to attend some kind of biblical studies with them. I was happy because it really would have been lonesome and maybe difficult for me to walk about the old city alone. I looked at this young 40 year old man of God, gratefully--he was sturdily built with wavy dark hair, combed back in the front and to the side, astonishing blue eyes and the goodness of a choir boy written across his face. I was sure the Lord had arranged for him to miss all the events at St. Ann's because I really needed somebody.

I began to learn that Jesus must have spent many hours on this hillside of the Mount of Olives as He talked with "them" about many things. It encompasses acres of land covered with trees and bushes. One or many persons could walk around the hillside and not be seen or noticed. I could clearly look down at the Temple site, now the Mosque, and see almost the whole city of Old Jerusalem.

I later learned more about the golden-domed Mosque of the Rock or Mosque of Omar. He was the Ommyad Caliph who built the marvelous shrine in 691 A.D., claiming that Mohammed made his Ascension into Heaven from the close-by silver-domed Mosque call El Aksa which means "the distant". The location is on Mt. Moriah, which is first mentioned in the Book of Genesis (Gen. 22:1-4), where Abraham was sent by God to the "land of Moriah" to offer up his sacrifice. Then two Temples had been built on Mount Moriah. Justinian had built a basilica in 550 in honor of St. Mary. So very much history in that walled-in-City that one can traverse by foot in one or two days.

Later, when I was reading about the historical Jesus, a Jewish writer, when mentioning Jesus of Nazareth, said "He often bivouacked with his disciples here". I had not realized that if you walked to the top of the Mount of Olives to Gethsemane, you would be at the place of Jesus' ascension into heaven. Gaeton suggested that we walk up there. We agreed to meet Faride at the shrine of the Ascension. We started the ascent about 11 a.m. The sun was hot as we climbed the steep narrow road. We could see that there were many churches marking different spots of Jesus' life on earth. First, after the Church of all Nations, we arrived at the Church of Mary Magdalene, a Russian -type church with mushroom domes, spear-like spires and a bell tower. A sign said it was closed today.

"Sometimes, I think that's the story of my life," I confided breathlessly to Gaeton as we continued our upward climb.

154

But, then we saw a little nun bustling about and she said we could view the grounds of the church. It was truly beautiful. The shrubbery up here was green and luxuriant, especially if comparing it with Arabia where I had been just two days ago, but not like my own Minnesota which is truly green and fertile in the summer. Still, this is desert land. The Israelites have somehow installed a kind of irrigating system here in Jerusalem that really works; thus they have cultivated the dry arid land.

We climbed the winding old stairway in the ancient mushroom-shaped bell tower and took pictures from the small window at the top -- a bird's eye view of Jerusalem. The Golden Gate is focused in the center of this particular little tower window where it had been prophesied in the Old Testament that the promised Messiah would ride through that gate into the city. Legend says it has been cemented up for centuries, I was told. The Jewish tradition holds that the Messiah will come through this gate during the last days to gather his own people. Therefore, the dearest wish of the Jewish person is to be buried as close to that gate (also called Gate of Mercy) as possible. They, of course, do not believe as the Christians do, that the Messiah already rode through this gate on a donkey 2000 years ago. Also, tradition says that a Turkish king, hearing that a King who would rule the world would ride through it, ordered it to be closed forever, so the prophecy would not come true. But, Christians firmly believe that it was already after the fact, citing the day Jesus, on the back of a donkey, rode into the city while the people laid palms in his path.

We began the steep ascent again. The sun was almost warm now and at one time I sat down to rest on a Jewish gravestone. I asked Gaeton to take my picture there. Then we traveled on. Up, up we walked and I couldn't help but look back every few minutes, not only to enjoy the marvelous panoramic view of Jerusalem, but to assure myself that I was really here looking at that marvelous City of Peace, the promised land of Moses, the hope and promise of all men who believe in the monolithic living God. The Israelites, Christians and Moslems all hold the belief of that one living God in common. Why, they must ever fight and kill, often in the name of God, is beyond my comprehension.

From here I see the Valley of Kidron, beyond that the walk and roadways that surround the wall, then the uneven structure of the wall itself. The top of the wall is straight and even, except for the side facing this Mount of Olives or Gethseman. The Dome of the Rock on the other side of the Golden Gate is spectacular. It still has porticos and ruins of Solomon's glorious Temple of centuries ago, but now is the Moslem's third most holy place on earth. To the left we could see the famous Jewish Wailing Wall where the Israelis pray.

"I can't believe it," I involuntarily sigh as I huff and puff on the steep narrow road. "I just can't believe I'm here in Jerusalem."

"I know what you mean, Claire," Gaeton said seriously. "The only reason I'm here is because my dear family and friends held a farewell party for me before I left and gave me gifts of money. It was enough so that I could make a side trip to the Holy Land for four days on my way back to Lilongue in Central Africa."

"I wish we knew the story behind everything we are seeing and everywhere we walk," I said as we trudged onward and upward.

"It would take many more days than either one of us has, to know all of that," he said. "I think every step we take here is on some historical site. I can't get over how so much of the Bible actually took place in this seemingly small bit of the earth," Gaeton said, also puffing as he trudged on the dusty road in the hot sun.

"How sad it is to be so totally unprepared for the greatest experience of my life," I commented. "You see, Gaeton, I didn't know I was coming to Jerusalem until three days ago, when Karl and Margaret gave me the airplane fare to get here, but I had to fly all the way to Athens and then from Athens to Tel-Aviv. Hardly anyone in Saudi Arabia has ever been to Israel. My brother couldn't even mention the word 'Jerusalem' to me as I left the airport in Jiddah yesterday morning. So, I knew nothing about coming here. I didn't even know that Tel-Aviv was so far from here. Thank God that I met you. What would I have done?" I leaned against the wall to rest a moment. The narrow road was very steep.

I am in the same place as you are," he answered in his French accent. "I decided to use the money from the going-away party that my neighbors gave to me to come here. That was just a few days before I left Canada."

I smiled at my friend, knowing I had been given a special grace when I met him.

We looked overhead and noted it must be noon because the sun was directly overhead in the clear blue sky. We continued to trudge up the hill and had to hug the wall to keep from being hit as a taxi zoomed by us. We caught a glimpse of Faride in the passenger seat waving and laughing at us as they drove on. The road was just wide enough for one car or bus (a bus had passed us loaded with a group of tourists). Finally we arrived at the summit of Gethsemane. To the right was a huge luxury hotel and to the left we saw the rounded dome of a small chapel. Faride Zahoor stood by this place with the driver of the taxi, waiting for us.

"This is the place of Jesus' ascension," Faride said and we went inside to see the footprint in the stone, purportedly Jesus's last step upon the earth. Faride waited outside impatiently, his hat pushed back puckishly on his abundant dark hair. His white shirt, tie and long top coat reminded me that, Faride, in his own way, was a top notch salesman, selling the story of Christianity sites to hungry Christians who long to walk in the same paths as their Savior.

Because of the shortage of time and Faride's impatience, before the importance of this special shrine even registered in my heart, we were out of the little chapel and climbing into the back seat of the taxi with Faride and the driver in the front. It was a relief to sit as we drove down the road we had laboriously ascended only minutes ago. Within two miles we were in Bethany.

"There is my house and the one next to it is also mine," Faride said proudly, as he dramatically removed the toothpick from his mouth and pointed to several houses on a hill across the road. Bethany was a surprisingly small village through which wound a narrow road, There were a few small shops, grazing goats and many rocks dotting the landscape. "I have five children, also," Faride added proudly.

Just outside the village we passed the tomb of Lazarus. The driver stepped on the brakes, almost passing it because it was hardly noticeable. We got out and descended a steep narrow stairway that wound deep into the musty rock tomb. The rickety narrow steps of stone became more and more tapering until I, who consider myself at least moderately brave, couldn't go down any further. I couldn't breathe. It may have been 50 feet deep, but Gaeton continued on down to the bottom. As I turned around to climb back up, with the dirt sides crowding in on me, I tried to imagine myself in the crowd of people of Bethany that historical day when Jesus called Lazarus back to life from the grave. To have been standing outside that tomb and perhaps hear the footsteps of that ghostly figure wrapped in yards and yards of linen cloth, emerging from that tomb surely must have created a disturbing wonder and fear in the hearts of those witnesses. Who could have attributed it to anything else than a miracle? How then could anyone deny the divinity of Jesus?

As we emerged from the cold tomb, an old woman stood there with her palm open for money, and amazingly Faride, who knew that Gaeton and I were both very low on funds, entreated us, "Give her a bit of money--she is old and poor and keeps up the tomb."

At this moment, it dawned on me that Faride was playing us for all we were worth. I asked myself, what could she possibly do to keep up this musty old hole in the ground? I shook my head, not understanding, except that Faride probably deals with all of these people, taxi drivers and others and pretends to be friends with people like us--how naive we are. I felt disillusioned, but later when I asked Gaeton if he was disappointed in Jerusalem and all of this 'selling' by so many people who weren't Christian. He said, "No, I'm not disappointed. One can take away with him whatever he wishes. To me it doesn't make any difference that many people must beg for their living here--except it is sad, that being Palestinians, it may be the only way they can make a living. This is still the land where Jesus lived and walked." I also adopted that philosophy myself right then, and will remember it forever, because Gaeton Poulin, the priest, was right. This was still the very land where He walked, lived, died and rose from the dead.

ARAB GUIDE, FARIDE ZAHOOR
AT ENTRANCE OF ASCENSION,
TOP OF THE GARDEN
OF GETHSEMANE

CLAIR RESTING ON JEWISH TOMB ON WAY TO GETHSEMANE NOT KNOWING
IT IS FORBIDDEN TO SIT ON THE GRAVES

THE LION'S GATE I.E. ST. STEPHEN'S GATE,
ENTRANCE TO ST. ANNE'S CHURCH

CHAPTER V

BETHLEHEM

Faride hurried us back into the taxi and the non-English speaking driver took us across the barren land toward Bethlehem. We could already see it on a distant hill just beyond Bethany. Faride did call our attention to a Palestinian camp on a hillside; a sad looking village of tents. People and kids poked around in the rubble. Even from a distance, the people looked dejected by the way they walked. Poverty and despair would have been my description. "The Israelis have thrown them out of their homes," Faride said sincerely. "The Jews need to expand, so they take over our homes and just throw us out."

I could hardly believe it, but I had met quite a few displaced Palestinians in my travels in the mideast and knew that they were daily bombed out of their homes and then again bombed in their tented hillside cities, too. I really felt for them and wished Americans could know the truth about these so called "retaliatory raids", the Israelis constantly held. Retaliatory for what? For living--for existing!

The road led south through the Valley of the Giants where the ancient Philistines were defeated twice by King David. Then Faride pointed out the "Well of the Magi" where the wise men rested when losing sight of the star, but then saw its reflection in the water and knew they were traveling in the right direction. Faride said, "We Arabs also believe that St. Mary, the mother of Jesus, rested here on her way to Bethlehem." The taxi driver had paused for a moment while Faride explained, then stomped on the gas and we whizzed off leaving a trail of dust on the winding ribbon road.

And ahead we could see the Monastery of St. Elijah on a hill which affords a commanding view from its roof of the blue mountains of Moab, the Dead Sea in the east and Bethlehem and Jerusalem on the north. We had hardly passed this monument to the past when we descended into a deep valley, which winds eastward to the Dead Sea which we could see off in the distance. And then we see a domed topped shrine or cenotaph, which Faride tells us is the legendary tomb of Rachael, the beloved wife of Jacob (Gen. 35: 16-29). I shake my head in wonderment, hardly believing the ancient sites. We in America cannot fathom the history of time immemorial because in relation, our nation is like a crawling baby in the span of time.

To the right is a large village of Beit-Jala mentioned in Isaiah. Samuel and Josh). The cab driver kicking up dust hardly gives us time to absorb it. When the road forks, it leads to the village of Hebron, but we continued on the main road into Bethlehem.

Already we were winding up the rocky hill approach to Bethlehem. In breathless wonder, we could see shepherds watching their sheep graze in the fields. The time gap of two thousand years unwrapped again. Only the car in which we rode had been added to the scenery from this time to that. Our car drove right up the cobblestone road into the midst of the Bazaar, that wonderful kind of market place indigenous to the mideast. The Bazaar faded into the background as Faride pointed out that right here in the heart of the small village was the Church of the Nativity. The taxi driver let us out right at the door and we had to bend our heads to enter in through the small door that opened into the famous birth place of Jesus Christ. Faride told us that it was built this small so that the Turks couldn't ride their camels into the shrine and desecrate it, as had happened many centuries ago. We walked down wide narrow stairs to the place of the nativity, now being taken care of by the Armenian Catholic Church priests. Gaeton and I both blessed ourselves in awe as we gazed at the beautiful altar of gold where the Savior had been born. Just think how our world would still be in darkness and our salvation uncertain, if right in this remote village, the promised Savior had not been born, I thought. Later, I knew that I would sit back and remember all of these most revered places--so much in such a short time was too much now for my mind to comprehend.

This beautiful marble altar has a huge gold star right in the middle of it proclaiming a wonderful message, "This is where Jesus Christ the Savior of the world was born". To the right is another altar under the auspices of the Roman Catholic Church where the wise men purportedly laid their gifts of gold, incense and myrrh for that unique child. These were grottoes, upstairs was the basilica itself. The walls down here were burned and old, marvelous testaments of its age. I can't describe the thoughts and feelings I burned with as I knelt in reverence here. Great gratitude overwhelmed me that I could be at this place. If only time weren't so short. We weren't allowed to linger. Already Faride was hurrying us along. Outside we walked up the cobblestones along which the bazaar or marketplace was located. We looked at the souvenirs in one or two of the open booths, but Faride literally steered us into a restaurant. It was true we were all very hungry. Again we hadn't eaten anything since early morning and it was now 2 p.m. We sat out on the veranda of the pleasant little restaurant and Faride grandly ordered a bottle of wine which the three of us shared. Chicken is on the menu, the only familiar word on it. It is the universal food. Gaeton and I ordered it. While we waited we looked out over Bethlehem and the surrounding countryside as we ate and chatted. I could see the minarets, the flat stone houses,the domes, the far mountains. The chicken was good, but when the bill came, Faride managed to disappear. Gaeton and I divided our meager funds to pay for his lunch. We both shrugged and paid for it, even though I still had half way around the world to travel and had hardly a dollar to my name.

The taxi was waiting outside. Faride, who reappeared just as quickly as he had disappeared, climbed in the front seat, Gaeton and I in the back. Down the hill we rumbled in that rather beat up vehicle, past the tomb of Jacob's beloved wife, Rachael, out through the hills where the shepherds were tending their sheep now as on the night of Jesus's birth. As through all the centuries--it was as if nothing had changed. Every inch of this land is part of the historical biblical past. In the distance we caught an occasional glimpse of the Dead Sea. As we approached Jerusalem, we saw the famous Western Wailing Wall where the Jews, wearing their little beanies, were praying. This wall is all that's left of the beautiful Temple razed by the Romans in 70 A.D., after having taken 47 years to build by Herod the Great. It was begun in 4 B.C. and finished in 42 A.D. I later read how beautiful it was and how the windowless room where the Holy of Holies, the Arc of the Covenant, was housed and was only entered once a year. The doors had been carved of olive wood, overlaid with gold.

This day we only glimpsed the great Dome of the Mosque, where the Moslems had built their third most sacred shrine right on the site of the Temple Mount. I tried to imagine that on this site, Jesus had been presented in the Temple when he was 40 days old, and then the time in between when He returned many times to celebrate the great feasts. Then the veil of the Temple that hid the Holy of Holies from the people was torn from top to bottom, maybe symbolizing the tearing down of the barriers between God and us, all of his human creatures.

As our taxi struggled up the hill to Gethsemane, I thought of how actually every inch of this land is embroiled in all kinds of history, good and bad, all within very close proximity. When we approached the Church of All Nations, a tall aging Priest met us at the door, expecting us. He stood near the garden where the gnarled old olive trees still guarded that place where Jesus spent so much of His time when He visited Jerusalem. We have long believed and read that He walked and rested there often with His Apostles. It was such a beautiful, green, blooming, restful place.

As we introduced ourselves to Father Godfrey, I thought of the legendary Friar Tuck of Robin hood lore. "I sometimes wake up in the morning and see this scene," he gestured over the city of Jerusalem below, "And I say to the Lord, 'why me, Lord, why am I so lucky in the last days of my life to look down on that beautiful golden Dome of the Rock where Solomon's Temple stood?" He asked us into the Church where the altar is built around the rock of the agony.

On this golden, memorable afternoon in February, the Jews and Arabs fought their embittered war on nearby Golan Heights, and the United States agonized over the outcome of the Watergate tapes. While the final destiny of President Nixon in the White house was being decided, Father Godfrey in his quiet corner of Gethsemane told us of the book he had written called, "The Fifth Gospel". "It may be irreverent of me to call it a Gospel," Father Godfrey said, looking out over the golden Dome of the Mosque into the City of Jerusalem, "But I strongly feel that Jerusalem and the land of Canaan itself, past and present, really is the fifth gospel".

"Will I be able to get a copy of it back in the States?" I asked.

"Yes, it's coming out in April in the United States," he said.

I made a mental note to order it as soon as I returned home.

The sun was very low in the sky already and it shone on that golden dome so brightly that it dazzled our eyes. But that universal globe of light peculiar to the whole world seemed to disappear fast over here. There was no prolonged sunset like we have in Minnesota. We said goodby to Father Godfrey thanking him for taking time to meet us. My second and last day was coming to its inevitable end. Along with our "friend" Faride Zahoor, Gaeton and I trudged down the road, past the Jewish graves where Faride told us was the most desired place on earth to be buried. "The Jews believe that the closer to the Golden Gate they are buried, the faster they will go to heaven on the final day," he explained airily waving his hand over the crowded hillside marked with marble gravestones, many of which had been pushed awry during the 1967 war with Syria. Those disturbed graves are a constant reminder of that war," Faride said of the Jews, himself being an Arab Moslem--i.e., a Palestinian. Straight as an eagle's flight, in front of all those graves, across the Kidron Valley and the busy highway outside the wall we only caught a hurried glimpse of the closed and cemented Golden Gate. So much

Faride asked us to come to Bethany with him and have supper in a little restaurant, but we declined, both of us realizing that Faride was ready for another free meal. I took his picture and said goodbye to him--he had been good to us.

CHAPTER VI

A FRIGHTENING RIDE

It was getting cold now and I was very tired. Gaeton and I climbed the hill outside the Golden Gate and sat down on those tombstones right outside the walls. I didn't realize until I got back home and read in a book that this was a Moslem burial ground and it is against the Moslem religion for anyone to sit or walk on their graves. We didn't know at that time. As evening closed in on us, the sun tinged the Dome of the Rock with golden rays. For the first time, Gaeton and I talked a little bit about our lives. We had both been so intent on making every moment count as we walked through the Holy City that we had spoken only of the biblical places we saw and the Lord. We had tried blindly to piece it all together because neither of us had any information to go on.

It was cooling very fast now, the sun dipped over the horizon as Gaeton told me of having contracted hepatitis while serving in his mission in Central Africa. He said that he walked around his mission with hepatitis for three years. He refused to lay down and be sick, and that kept him from getting well. "But there was so much to be done, so many people to serve, I couldn't lay down and rest," he stated earnestly.

Finally his Father Superior insisted he return to his home in Quebec. He spent a year recuperating and resting. He told me of how he stayed on his family farm, which was now deserted since his father died. Gaeton's eyes lit up as he spoke, his French accent so thick that I strained to understand his words. He told me of how he hunted, fished and visited his brothers and sisters who lived nearby the old homestead. Also he had two brothers who live in the States, Poughkeepsie, New York.

"I had time to think and sort out my mind during that year," he said.. "But now I feel well and renewed and very anxious to be back with my people in Africa. I am so busy there helping the people do everything in their lives. I miss them very much," he said simply. As I listened and looked into the eyes of this fine young man of God, I thought how good the Lord was to send Father Gaeton Poulin to me yesterday. It seemed so predestined when I think of it now, how we two were the only ones who missed the bus to Jerusalem. It couldn't have been coincidence. I had been so alone and so needful of a companion. This priest's goodness was an inspiration.

Entering St. Stephen's Gate now, where the first Christian martyr Stephen was stoned to death, I shivered in the coolness of the dark evening. It may have been 40 degrees. Gaeton's supper was scheduled for 7:30 with the other priests at St. Anne's. He agreed to help me find a place to eat, meanwhile running inside St. Anne's to put on a jacket. When he returned he carried his topcoat for me to put on. I had worn only a sweater when I came to old Jerusalem in the early morning.

As I stood waiting for his return, I realized it would have been difficult for me to be alone here. I watched the dark-complected white-gowned men pass by. I did have one frightening incident a little later while on my way to my room.

Meanwhile, we walked by a small restaurant. It didn't look too much different than other small cafes anywhere in the world. They even had hamburgers, miracle of miracles, first place since I left home. Only a few people were in the small eating place and as we waited for my order, we talked about his imminent return to Africa and my return to my life in the States. I promised to send him my slides when they were developed because I had taken many films of pictures. He didn't have a camera. After eating the very bad tasting piece of meat, we went out into the darkness of the night. We found a hostel where I could cash my very last traveler's check. We then saw some taxicabs outside of Herod's Gate. The drawbridge distinguished it from the other gates. Each one is distinguished by its own peculiarities. The other gates are: Zion Gate, Jaffa Gate, New Gate, Damascus Gate, St. Stephen's Gate (or the Lion's Gate), the Golden Gate (cemented closed) and the Dung Gate.

I handed the driver my destination address on a piece of

167

paper. He motioned me to climb in the passenger seat beside him. I watched my priest-friend walk over the drawbridge back into the wall of Jerusalem. He waved as he disappeared. As the cab pulled away I looked behind for my last glance at that city from which emanates so many of our beliefs and heritage. The night was coal-black as the cab wound down the hill toward New Jerusalem. I tried to make conversation with this Palestinian driver who didn't speak English. It was a mistake on my part, I soon found. I asked him if he knew Faride Zahoor. He recognized the name and suddenly became very agitated. He turned excitedly toward me and asked a question in broken English, "You pay for Faride's lunch, you pay taxi fare? Pay for wine?"

Hesitantly, I said yes, not knowing where this conversation was going. I also suddenly saw Faride in a new light, a real con artist who found people to help and then had them pay for all his daily fare.

The taxi driver was doing something very strange. He pulled dollar bills out of his stockings, wads of money from his pants and every place--in both hands he waved all this money while I thought of how I didn't know if I had enough to get out of my hotel room.

"You go with me to Jericho?" he asked loudly. "I got lots money!" He leaned toward me in the dark. I looked outside into the blackness of the night. I was very frightened at this moment. I had no idea where I was and no one in the whole world even knew I was here in Jerusalem, except Karl and he couldn't even mention the word in Saudi Arabia. I had been safe all this time, but now I didn't know how to handle this situation. "Eat, dance--Jericho--I got lots money," he repeated angrily as if the name of Faride set him off.

"No," I answered firmly. "America tomorrow." He shouted more angry than ever. I feared then that he wouldn't take me back to Har Aviv. He swung daringly around corners, past dark houses and through business districts. At least we were now in the city. I held my breath and prayed. More dangerous turns, more anger--"Go to Jericho with me," he muttered in the dark. Then, thank God, the taxi stopped abruptly. I was at my destination. "Ten pounds," he muttered.

"No, only seven pounds, " I said thinking of my shrinking funds.

"Ten pounds," he stated ominously. For this moment, I knew I had to be grateful to be here safely at my "hotel". I gave ten pounds and fled toward the house.

"You had your chance," he called threateningly after me as I ran up the road, past the three houses in the front of the yard, to the one I had really only seen in the dark these past two nights. I sighed in relief as I closed the front door behind me. I thought of how I had sent a postcard to my family from Athens just two days ago saying I was going to Jerusalem, but I knew it wouldn't arrive for at least a week. Other than that no one would check on my whereabouts. The thought was sobering, but then when one comes to the Lord's Holy City, one cannot bring fear with her, I told myself.

Just then the landlady's daughter came out of their apartment and said, "My mother isn't home tonight, but she left the bill with me seeing you are leaving at a quarter to six in the morning." She handed me the bill and I told her I'd come downstairs and square up with her shortly.

Back in my austere room, I ran hot bath water into that lovely bathtub and couldn't wait to climb in and get warm. I shivered from the cold. It was very early spring in Israel, whereas in Arabia, it was about 75 degrees at this time of night and in the 80's during the day. My room was icy cold, but I turned on the heat and it began to warm up.

After this wonderful warming bath, I suddenly noticed that the coat I had hung over the back of the chair belonged to Gaeton Poulin. I gasped. I had completely forgotten that I had worn it. I counted my money and found that with money and checks and whatever the landlady would accept, it took my last cent to pay my bill which meant I didn't have enough money to pay another taxi driver to take it back to him. Besides, I was so exhausted that I couldn't have made that half hour trip across the dark area again.

Going downstairs to pay my bill, I asked to use the phone

to call Gaeton at St. Anne's. The phone rang again and again. Their system is antiquated compared to our modern telephone companies. Finally a voice answered, sounding very far off. It was Gaeton himself. He said he had been resting because he was scheduled to leave at 4:30 a.m. to go to Nazareth on a bus. It is apparently a bit of a trip. "It's all right about the coat," he said, but I knew he needed it --and he probably wouldn't have the money to replace it for a long time. I told him I hoped he was coming this way and could get it. He said he doubted it, but I told him I'd leave it with the landlady's daughter with a prayer. I couldn't think of how else to get it to him. Later I found that he had walked all that way and picked it up.

Now, I had to write my diary notes even though it was late. This day had been vitally important in my life's experiences and I had to preserve the memories. By the time I wrote, packed and climbed into bed, it was almost 2 a.m. The landlady had lent me an alarm clock. I set it for 4:15, but I was so exhausted and so deep in sleep that I turned it off in the darkness of the morning and rolled over. Suddenly something popped in my head and I woke up with a start. It was 4:40 already. Panic stricken, I threw my things in my suitcase, dressed and rushed outside into the inky darkness of the hours before the dawn, hoping I hadn't forgotten something important. I looked about anxiously. There was absolutely no life anywhere. Had I missed the charute taxi? I had no way to know only that I was late getting to the corner. I shivered, it was so cold. No luxuries, like street lights. They didn't exist in this part of the City. Anxiety and fear gripped my heart. If I missed it, I couldn't possibly make the plane and I had run out of money. I felt very forlorn. Here, there was only hostility from the landlady. What would I do? I waited and peered into the darkness, praying I would see an approaching vehicle.

And then suddenly lights loomed out of the darkness. I held my breath--it stopped. It was a limousine. The driver got out and opened the door for me. I climbed into the last of the seven seats. There are no words to describe my relief at that moment. i could have kissed that driver, but not even one word was exchanged. We drove off. The other passengers were ghostlike figures in the dark. I couldn't see the wasteland between Tel -Aviv and Jerusalem where the relics of the 1967 clash with Syria are still painful reminders to the Jews of the seven day war that took place there.

The dawn came slowly on this strange 70 mile ride. The appearance of the sun cast an unearthly glow as it rose, a yellow globe on the horizon. It was hard to realize there were six other people in the car--they were all so quiet! When someone did speak, they spoke in soft voices and strange tongues. I could have pinched myself to see if this almost miraculous once-in-a-lifetime trip was really happening to me.

The ride seemed endless that early morning as the charute taxi took me away from Jerusalem, the city we all aspire to visit in our lifetime, like the Moslems aspire to visit Mecca. But Christians are not mandated to make the pilgrimage. The airport seemed small compared to some of the others--more like Duluth, not Chicago. Dawn was breaking in the east as we alighted from the bus. I immediately headed across the street, or square, to the place where my suitcases, heavy-laden with memorabilia from Jiddah, Saudi Arabia, were stored in a locker.

I managed to carry the heavily-laden suitcases across the street and into the airport, but I wasn't prepared for the ordeal I had to face when departing from Israel. Coming in had been easy, but the custom officials were very interested in my souvenirs from Arabia on my pending departure. It must have been not only unusual, but almost impossible for an American or anyone else to travel from Arabia to Israel. They were very curious and suspicious of me, a traveler who had circumvented the rules. The two customs agents opened both my suitcases as wide as they would go and proceeded to unwrap and inspect each thing thoroughly: the sea shells from the Red Sea that Rodion Rathbone had bequeathed to me; several brass camels; a bedouin camel whip with a hidden nail-sharp dagger in the handle; a round brass 100 year calendar; seed beads that resemble our rosary beads; small hubbly bubbly pipe that Arabian men smoke without tobacco; a velvet wall hanging of the Kaaba, the great shrine in Mecca; etc. As agents examined each piece, always searching for hidden contraband, the two unsmiling inspectors asked, "Why did you buy this thing or that--did you bring messages to anyone in Israel? Do you know anyone in Jerusalem? Did you look anyone up? Did you bring anything into the country to deliver?" I shook my head to every question. After an interminable time in apprehensive anticipation there at the customs desk, I was allowed to pass on into the personal inspection room. The woman frisked me and finally passed me through. All passengers headed for Athens on the giant Boeing 747 were also personally inspected. The sun was now rising higher in the sky as I boarded the jet plane. Within fifteen minutes, the giant bird lifted into the heavens. I hadn't seen all of the Holy Land, but then I hadn't asked the Holy Spirit to see it all--I only had said, "I'd like to go to Jerusalem." The longer I live, the more I realize one has to be very careful and specific about what they ask for. I felt satisfied that morning that I had visited the Holy City. I settled back in my seat to consider all that had transpired these past days.

THE END